I WISH I
KNEW THAT

Written by Steve Martin,
Dr Mike Goldsmith and Marianne Taylor
Illustrated by Andrew Pinder
Edited by Elizabeth Scoggins

Designed by Zoe Bradley
Cover Illustrated by Hui Skipp
Cover Designed by Angie Allison

I WISH I
KNEW THAT

Buster Books

This paperback edition first published in 2016

First published in Great Britain in 2010 by Buster Books,
an imprint of Michael O'Mara Books Limited,
9 Lion Yard, Tremadoc Road, London SW4 7NQ

 www.busterbooks.co.uk Buster Children's Books  @BusterBooks

Every reasonable effort has been made to acknowledge all copyright holders. Any errors or omissions that may have occurred are inadvertent, and anyone with any copyright queries is invited to write to the publishers, so that a full acknowledgement may be included in subsequent editions of this work.

A CIP catalogue record for this book is available from the British Library.

ISBN: 978–1–78055–466–2

3 5 7 9 10 8 6 4 2

Printed and bound in January 2018 by CPI Group (UK) Ltd,
108 Beddington Lane, Croydon, CR0 4YY, United Kingdom.

Papers used by Michael O'Mara Books are natural, recyclable products made from wood grown in sustainable forests. The manufacturing processes conform to the environmental regulations of the country of origin.

CONTENTS

GETTING AHEAD
OF THE CLASS

Have you ever known something the other kids in your class didn't? Cool, isn't it?

In this book you will discover lots of exciting things your teachers haven't mentioned (and some of the things they have).

Find out the names of all the countries in the world and their capital cities. Discover how a black hole works and if a cold war really is cold. Read about an enormous island of floating plastic in the Pacific Ocean.

There are lots of bite-sized chunks of information from history and geography, to maths and science. There are even sections on literature and language, to make sure you get things right when you write.

Rather than a whole pile of books, you can get a taste of all these different subjects with just this one. In no time at all, you'll be able to impress your friends and family with a hundred interesting titbits. Better still, you'll stay way ahead of your classmates!

LITERATURE STUFF

SHAKESPEARE, IN SHORT

William Shakespeare, or the Bard (meaning poet), wrote some of the world's best-known plays and poems. He wrote funny plays known as comedies and sad plays, which are called his tragedies. Several plays are known as 'problem plays', which are very entertaining, but are neither comedies nor tragedies. Here are some brief introductions to his most famous plays to help you bluff your way through until you can see them at the theatre yourself.

Hamlet

Hamlet, the Prince of Denmark, is a troubled young man. His father, the king, has been murdered, and his mother has married his father's brother, Claudius, after only a few weeks.

One night, the ghost of the king appears to Hamlet and reveals that Claudius murdered him. He asks Hamlet to seek revenge, but Hamlet wants to find more proof of the murder first. To do this, he pretends to be driven mad by grief, and puts on a play for Claudius that tells the story of a murder similar to that of the king's. It makes it very clear that the king has been murdered by his brother. When Claudius reacts nervously to the play, Hamlet is convinced he is guilty.

Hamlet goes to confront his mother in her room, but he thinks he can hear Claudius hiding behind a curtain and stabs at him. Sadly, he has not killed Claudius, he has murdered Polonius, the father of Ophelia, a girl Hamlet once loved. The news drives Ophelia mad and she drowns herself.

These terrible events lead to more revenge and this time Polonius' son, Laertes (pronounced 'layer-tees'), decides to punish Hamlet. Claudius sets up a duel between Hamlet and

Laertes, but he gives Laertes a poisoned sword to make sure that Hamlet dies. Laertes fatally stabs Hamlet, but during the fight, the two men accidentally switch weapons and Hamlet also wounds Laertes with the poisoned sword.

A wounded Hamlet then manages to stab Claudius, but at that moment his mother drinks from the poisoned wine that Hamlet had prepared for Claudius. Laertes, Hamlet, his mother and Claudius all die – not really a happy ending.

Romeo And Juliet

This is the story of a young couple from two rival families, the Montagues and the Capulets. Romeo and Juliet fall in love instantly when they meet at Juliet's family party, and are later secretly married by Friar Laurence. However, Tybalt, a cousin of Juliet's, is angry that Romeo came to the party uninvited and challenges him to fight. When Romeo refuses, his friend Mercutio fights instead and is killed. Romeo murders Tybalt in revenge and is sent away as a punishment, leaving Juliet behind.

This wouldn't be so bad, except that Juliet's family, who still have no idea that she is married, arrange a wedding between Juliet and her cousin, Count Paris. To avoid Juliet getting stuck with a second husband she doesn't want, Friar Laurence comes up with a plan.

The plan involves Juliet drinking a potion to make her appear to be dead. The idea is that Romeo will come back and rescue her from her tomb. Sadly, for both Romeo and Juliet the plan goes disastrously wrong when a message, reassuring Romeo that Juliet is only sleeping in the tomb, gets lost. Poor Romeo returns home believing his wife is dead. Stricken with grief, he kills himself, and when Juliet wakes up she kills herself, too.

The Montagues and Capulets finally decide to stop being enemies, but it's all too late for Romeo and Juliet.

Now that's what you call a tragedy.

Much Ado About Nothing

On the way home from battle, Don Pedro, a prince, and his men, Claudio and Benedick, are invited to stay in Messina by the governor of the city, Leonato. Claudio is reunited with Leonato's daughter, Hero, who he once loved. Claudio and Hero are driven crazy by the constant arguing between Beatrice (Leonato's niece) and Benedick. They decide to trick Beatrice into believing Benedick loves her and to convince Benedick that Beatrice loves him. Meanwhile, Don Pedro's evil brother, Don John, tricks Claudio into thinking Hero loves someone else. Claudio is so angry that he even abandons Hero on their wedding day.

Eventually, Claudio discovers the truth about Hero and, as Benedick and Beatrice have indeed fallen in love, the four of them decide on a double wedding.

Macbeth

People often call this the 'Scottish play' rather than saying the name 'Macbeth' out loud. This is because, traditionally, the play is said to be unlucky. Superstitious actors hope to avoid any accidents by not mentioning the 'M' word.

As the play begins, Macbeth and his friend Banquo, both generals for King Duncan of Scotland, meet three witches – the 'weird sisters'. They tell Macbeth that he will be made thane (a nobleman) of Cawdor, and then become king. However, they also tell his friend Banquo that his sons will be kings, not Macbeth's. When Macbeth becomes a thane, he and his scheming wife, Lady Macbeth, decide to kill King Duncan to hurry the witches' predictions along. Even when Macbeth is king he is not satisfied, as he knows that Banquo's sons will inherit the throne, instead of his own children. So he has Banquo killed, although Banquo's son escapes. Banquo's ghost then drives Lady Macbeth mad, and she dies.

The weird sisters give Macbeth another prophecy – that he will be safe until Birnham Wood comes to Dunsinane (Macbeth's castle). This seems so impossible that Macbeth believes his position as king is secure. However, King Duncan's son, Malcolm, brings his army, camouflaged with branches from Birnham Wood and Macbeth is killed.

Othello

This play shows how jealousy can make a mess of a great romance. Othello, a brave general, falls in love with and secretly marries Desdemona, the daughter of a senator. However, an enemy is soon plotting against him.

When Othello promotes a young soldier named Cassio to lieutenant over Iago, a more experienced soldier, Iago is furious. He gets revenge by convincing Othello that Desdemona is having a relationship with Cassio. Iago makes sure that Othello overhears Cassio discussing his love for a woman and Othello assumes that it must be his wife, Desdemona. Othello's anger gets worse when Desdemona's handkerchief (planted by Iago) is found in Cassio's rooms.

Othello is so jealous that he ends up killing Desdemona, even though she has done nothing wrong. When Iago's trickery is revealed, Othello is devastated and kills himself.

So, if you fall in love, remember the play's warning – jealousy is a 'green-eyed monster'.

The Tempest

A powerful wizard named Prospero and his daughter, Miranda, were cast adrift at sea by his brother, Antonio. For twelve years they have been stuck on a magical island with two servants – a spirit named Ariel, and Caliban, the half-human son of a witch.

With the help of the King of Naples, Alonso, Antonio stole Prospero's title of Duke of Milan. The play begins with a violent storm (a 'tempest') conjured by Prospero to destroy Antonio and Alonso's ship, which is sailing past the island.

Once the survivors of the shipwreck have struggled to shore, Ariel helps Prospero take his revenge, tormenting Antonio and Alonso. In the meantime, Alonso's son, Ferdinand, has met and fallen in love with Miranda.

Eventually, Prospero, Antonio and Alonso manage to mend their differences. Prospero gets his title back, and they all leave the island together. A favourable wind (a final gift from Ariel) speeds them home, where Miranda and Ferdinand marry, uniting the kingdoms of Milan and Naples.

POETS' CORNER

Poetry is everywhere – in the songs you hear on the radio and in the advertising slogans you see on TV. Here is a selection of some of the most well-known poets in history, with examples of their poems that you may enjoy.

William Shakespeare
(Born 1564, died 1616)

Best known for his plays, Shakespeare was also a great poet, writing more than 100 sonnets (14-line poems), including the famous love poem that begins, 'Shall I compare thee to a Summer's day?'

Samuel Taylor Coleridge
(Born 1772, died 1834)

Coleridge's most famous poem – the mysterious and scary *The Rime of the Ancient Mariner* – tells the story of a sailor who kills a large bird called an albatross, and then suffers terribly for his crime.

Edward Lear
(Born 1812, died 1888)

As well as his famous poem 'The Owl and The Pussy Cat', Lear created bizarre characters for his poems such as the Pobble (who had no toes), the Quangle-Wangle (with a marvellous hat), and the Dong (with a luminous nose).

Walt Whitman
(Born 1819, died 1892)

An American poet, Whitman spent much of his life working on his poetry collection, *Leaves of Grass*. He kept releasing new versions of the book until he died.

Rudyard Kipling
(Born 1865, died 1936)

Author of *The Jungle Book* and *Just So Stories*, Kipling was also a brilliant poet. His poem 'If' was chosen as Britain's favourite poem in 1995.

T. S. Eliot
(Born 1888, died 1965)

As well as his poems for adults such as *The Wasteland*, Eliot wrote a book of poems for children, called *Old Possum's Book of Practical Cats*, which was the inspiration for a famous musical called *Cats*.

Wilfred Owen
(Born 1893, died 1918)

Owen was a soldier in the First World War and his poems, including 'Anthem for Doomed Youth', show his anger about the horrors of war. Owen was killed in 1918, just one week before the war ended.

John Betjeman
(Born 1906, died 1984)

Betjeman's poetry is full of fondness for a time gone by. Written with a lot of humour, his poems contain references to potting sheds, tennis, marmalade, the seaside and railways. For example, in the poem 'Harrow-on-the-Hill', he describes this area, in northwest London, as an ocean of rooftops, with the noise of the trains sounding like waves.

CLASSIC READS

In any bookshop or library you'll discover tales of magic and fantasy, pirates and shipwrecks, of things that happened long ago and of adventures from far away. The only trouble you may have is deciding which book to read first. Here is a quick guide to some of the most exciting reads from children's literature that you should be able to find easily.

If you read and enjoy these books, there are suggestions of other books you might also like below each one.

The Wonderful Wizard Of Oz
(By L. Frank Baum)

When people think of *The Wizard of Oz*, they may think of the film musical, but the novel that came first is worth reading, too. You'll discover lots of things that aren't in the film at all. Something that may surprise you is that L. Frank Baum wrote 15 books about Oz, so there are many more to enjoy. In this first book, just as in the film, Dorothy is whisked away from her home in Kansas by a tornado. She lands in a strange land called Oz, where she travels with the Tin Woodman, the Cowardly Lion and the Scarecrow. Only if she can reach the Emerald City and find the Wizard of Oz will Dorothy be able to get home.

You could try: *The Lion, the Witch and the Wardrobe* by C. S. Lewis.

The Call Of The Wild
(By Jack London)

A dog named Buck is taken from
a comfortable life on a farm
and sent to the frozen north
to haul a dog sled. Buck adapts
quickly and is soon leader of
the sled team. However, when
the dogs are sold to a group of
inexperienced men searching for
gold, things do not go well.

A man named John Thornton
rescues Buck and they form a strong friendship, although Buck
finds the 'call of the wild' (his natural instincts) hard to resist.

You could try: *Stig of the Dump* by Clive King.

Moonfleet
(By J. Meade Faulkner)

Fifteen-year-old John Trenchard lives in
a fishing village named Moonfleet. He
and Elzevir, a smuggler, find the pirate
Blackbeard's lost diamond. However,
they are tricked out of it, arrested and
sentenced to life in prison for trying to
steal it back.

After 10 years in prison, the two are
put on a ship and a terrible storm
provides an opportunity to escape that
they can't pass up.

You could try: *The Eagle of the Ninth*
by Rosemary Sutcliff.

The Adventures Of Tom Sawyer
(By Mark Twain)

In a village in the American South, next to the Mississippi River, Tom and his friends are always misbehaving. When they become pirates and sail away to an island in the middle of the river, their families think they've drowned. The boys sneak home and reappear at their own funeral! However, things become much more serious when Tom and his friend, Huckleberry Finn, witness a murder.

You could try: *Adventures of Huckleberry Finn* by Mark Twain.

Anne Of Green Gables
(By L. M. Montgomery)

A grown-up brother and sister called Matthew and Marilla Cuthbert send to an orphanage for a boy to help on their farm, called Green Gables. When a girl named Anne arrives instead, they let her stay. Matthew and Marilla grow to love Anne, but her vivid imagination soon gets her into trouble. Anne competes with a boy named Gilbert Blythe to be top of the class at school, which leads to some of the best tantrums ever written.

You could try: *Pollyanna* by Eleanor H Porter.

The Wind In The Willows
(By Kenneth Grahame)

When Mole visits a river for the first time, he makes friends with Ratty, Toad and Badger. In the first of many adventures, Toad is arrested and sent to prison for stealing a motor car. He manages to escape in disguise, but when he returns home he finds that his house, Toad Hall, has been taken over by a group of ferrets and weasels. He and his friends gather together to recapture Toad Hall.

You'll never see your local riverbank in the same way again!

You could try: *Tarka the Otter* by Henry Williamson.

The Jungle Book
(By Rudyard Kipling)

This collection of stories includes 'Mowgli's Brothers', which became the classic animated film, *The Jungle Book*. This particular story tells of a young boy brought up in the jungle with characters such as Shere Khan – a tiger determined to kill him, Bagheera – a wise panther, Baloo – a lazy old bear, and Kaa – a cunning python.

Other stories include 'Rikki-tikki-tavi', an action-packed tale about a mongoose who saves a family from cobras, and 'Toomai of the Elephants', about a young boy who witnesses the magical sight of a legendary elephant dance.

You could try: *Watership Down* by Richard Adams.

The Adventures Of Pinocchio
(By Carlo Collodi)

A man named Geppetto is given a piece of wood by Master Cherry the carpenter. He carves it into a puppet and names him Pinocchio. Little Pinocchio turns out to be very mischievous for a puppet, and gets himself into lots of scrapes throughout the story. Even if you have seen the cartoon version of *Pinocchio*, there's much more to discover in the original book. It takes being turned into a donkey, being swallowed by a shark, and Geppetto falling ill, for Pinocchio to realize, with the help of the Blue Fairy, that the better he behaves, the better his reward.

You could try: *Skellig* by David Almond.

Treasure Island
(By Robert Louis Stevenson)

In one of the most famous swashbuckling tales ever, young Jim Hawkins finds a treasure map and sets sail on the *Hispaniola* to find the treasure. While at sea, Jim discovers that the ship's cook, Long John Silver, and many of the crew are pirates. When they reach the island, the double-crossing and violence begins.

You could try:
Twenty Thousand Leagues Under the Sea by Jules Verne.

Little Women
(By Louisa May Alcott)

The author based this story on her own family life. It tells the story of four sisters, Meg, Jo, Beth and Amy March. Set at the time of the American Civil War, the girls' father is away working as a chaplain for the army. The March sisters are poor, but they make the best of what they have. The story follows them as they grow and have many adventures and romances.

You could try:
Emma by Jane Austen.

MUSIC AND ART STUFF

A BRIEF HISTORY OF MUSIC

The history of classical music in Europe and the Americas can be divided into several periods, each with different styles and often with well-known stars. Jump right in with this brief guide to some of the most important periods.

Medieval

Most music that is still known from this period is religious – in particular Gregorian chants, which are named after the 6th-century Pope, Gregory. These were written in 'plainsong', which means that everyone sings the same tune together.

Renaissance

During the Middle Ages, a lot of the knowledge that had been gained from the Greeks and Romans was lost. The Renaissance (which means rebirth) began in Italy in the 14th century, and was a time of rediscovery. People began to think about science, art and culture again, and music became a more important part of entertainment as well as of religion. Even King Henry VIII of England wrote music. Between marrying, divorcing and beheading wives, Henry wrote his own, catchy folksongs (but he didn't compose *Greensleeves*, as many people say).

Baroque

By the Baroque period (roughly 1600 to 1750), instrument

makers had developed sophisticated musical instruments. This meant that composers, such as Handel, Vivaldi and Bach, could write even more interesting music. Vivaldi, who wrote hundreds of pieces, is familiar to many people because of his violin concerto, *The Four Seasons*, which conveys the feeling of each of the seasons in a year.

Classical

The Classical period went from the mid-18th century to around 1820. Top composers of the age included Mozart, Haydn, Schubert and Beethoven. Beethoven gradually lost his hearing. He was completely deaf for the last few years of his life, but he continued to write music. When his *Ninth Symphony* was performed for the first time in 1824, Beethoven had no idea how much people were applauding until a musician made him turn to look at the audience.

Romantic

Beethoven's third symphony, 'Eroica', which he completed in 1804 was the first Romantic symphony. By the time he died in 1827, the Romantic period was fully under way and lasted into the 20th century. Composers such as Strauss, Verdi and Puccini were able to make money from their music because it was so popular. Skilled solo musicians, including a man named Paganini, also became superstars of the day. People even described him as a 'devil' because he could play such incredibly difficult music.

20th Century

Among many great 20th-century composers, such as Prokofiev, Shostakovich, Gershwin and Copland, is Igor Stravinsky, a Russian composer, who wrote the music for many popular ballets. One of these – *The Rite of Spring* – caused a riot at its first performance in Paris.

THE WORLD OF ART

In the history of art, there have been many different 'movements' (when groups of artists have worked in similar styles). Here are some of the most well-known to start you off. So next time you're walking around an art gallery, you can impress everyone with your superior knowledge.

Renaissance

In the same way that the Renaissance was important to the world of music (see page 24), it also gave much more freedom to painters and sculptors. Renewed interest in the ancient world made the subjects of science, literature and art very popular. Leonardo da Vinci, who excelled in them all, is one of the most famous people of the Renaissance.

Florence, in Italy, was the centre of Renaissance art for two centuries. A powerful family called the Medici who lived there were patrons to artists including Michelangelo. He is known for his painting on the ceiling of the Sistine Chapel in the Vatican.

Baroque And Rococo

In the 17th century, artists such as Caravaggio developed the Baroque style – a grand and dramatic way of painting that influenced the designs of buildings at the time, too.

YOU KNOW WHAT? I'VE GONE OFF IT.

Baroque lasted until the 18th century, when it developed into the Rococo period – a more delicate and decorative style used by artists such as Canaletto.

Romanticism

In the 1800s, many artists – Constable, Turner and Blake, for example – developed a more 'romantic' style. This meant that their paintings were more colourful and wild than those before, which had been painted following strict rules.

Arts And Crafts

In the 1850s, Victorians were used to very over-the-top decoration and ornaments in their homes. The development of factories meant that these objects could be made in large numbers. However, artists such as William Morris preferred objects to be simple, well-made and handcrafted.

Impressionism

In the 19th century in France, a group of artists that included Monet and Degas developed new ideas about painting. They used colour in a different way to capture an 'impression' of objects and scenes, rather than painting them to look like photographs. For example, instead of painting a blue flower using only blue paint, they might add areas of dark purple in the shadows or pale orange where light reflected on the edge of a petal.

Expressionism

In the late 19th and early 20th century, Expressionist artists such as Edvard Munch often exaggerated the shapes and colours of the things they painted to show how they felt at the time, or how they felt about a particular subject. Munch, for example, painted a famous picture called 'The Scream', which is full of bright, swirling colours and shows a person holding their head and looking extremely unhappy!

LANGUAGE STUFF

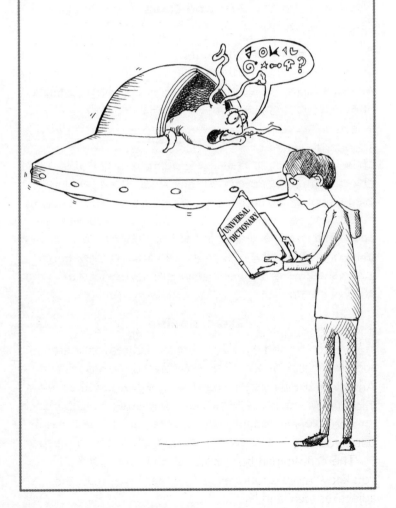

THE PARTS OF SPEECH

The names of the different jobs that words do are called the 'parts of speech'. There are eight of them:

Nouns

Nouns are naming words. Some nouns name particular people or places (your friend 'John' or the planet 'Earth', for example) and are called 'proper nouns'. They start with a capital letter.

Anything that is a kind of person ('boy', 'parent'), a kind of place ('city', 'countryside') or a kind of thing ('book', 'television') is called a common noun. Some nouns describe a group of people or things, such as a 'team' or a 'pack'. These are called collective nouns. Not all nouns name objects that you can see. Words such as 'Tuesday' and 'happiness' are also nouns.

Verbs

Verbs are often called 'doing words'. They tell you what a person or thing is doing or being. 'To run', 'to give', 'to cook', 'to be' and 'to talk' are all verbs. (When a verb is written out including the word 'to' at the beginning it is called the 'infinitive'.)

Adjectives

An adjective describes a noun and gives you extra information about it. For instance, you could just say,
   'The woman bought a car,'
but if you say,
   'The *rich* woman bought a *fast* car,'
you know more about her and her car because of the adjectives 'rich' and 'fast'.

Adverbs

Adverbs describe verbs and give you more information about what is going on. The sentence,

'The rich woman drives the car,'

will do, but,

'The rich woman drives the car *carefully*,'

gives more detail.

Many adverbs answer the questions 'How?', 'When?', 'Where?', or 'Why?' and many of them end in '-ly'. 'Carefully', 'quickly', 'quietly' and 'loudly' are all adverbs.

You can also use adverbs to describe adjectives. In the sentence,

'The *incredibly* rich woman drives carefully,'

the word 'incredibly' tells you how rich the woman is (very).

Adverbs can even be used to describe other adverbs, as in the sentence,

'The incredibly rich woman drives *quite* carefully.'

Now we know that perhaps the woman doesn't drive as carefully as she should (and you will also have spotted that 'quite' is one of those adverbs that doesn't end in '-ly').

Pronouns

A pronoun ('I', 'you', 'he', 'she', 'it', 'we', 'us', 'they' and 'them') replaces a noun in a sentence, so that you don't have to keep repeating the noun. Rather than saying,

'The woman drives the car every day and washes the car once a week,'

try,

'The woman drives the car every day and washes *it* once a week.'

'It' replaces the word car.

The words 'mine', 'yours', 'its', 'his', 'hers', 'ours' and 'theirs' are what are called possessive pronouns. They are used to show who owns something, as in the sentence,

'I took the book because it was *mine*'.

Conjunctions

You use conjunctions, or connecting words, all the time to join different parts of a sentence together (more on these on pages 33–34). They join words, phrases and clauses.

The word 'and' is the conjunction you use most often, but there are many more, including 'or', 'but', 'nor', 'yet' and 'so'.

Prepositions

Prepositions are words that go before nouns in sentences. They show the relationship of one thing to another. Rather helpfully, a preposition tells you where something is – its position. There are quite a few, but the ones you'll see most are 'by', 'to', 'in', 'into', 'for', 'from', 'of', 'between', 'with' and 'on'. So you could say,

'The woman got *in* her car, *with* her friends and went *to* the shops.'

Interjections

An interjection is a word that shows strong feelings, such as excitement or surprise. An interjection will often have an exclamation mark after it (especially if something is particularly exciting or surprising). Examples include, 'Wow!', 'Ouch!' and 'Hurray!'

HEY! LISTEN TO ME.

Did You Know?

'The' is the definite article. It tells you about a particular thing. 'A' is the indefinite article – it could be any one of those things. For example, in the sentence,

'The boy loved *the* dog and his friend wanted *a* dog, too,'

you can tell that the boy loved one particular dog, but his friend who would like a dog doesn't necessarily want *that* dog.

PUTTING A SENTENCE TOGETHER

You probably already know, of course, that a sentence begins with a capital letter and ends with a full stop (or a question mark or an exclamation mark). It's what goes between the capital letter and the full stop that can cause confusion. Writing in clear sentences is the best possible way to make sure that your writing makes sense to your readers (whether it's your teachers or the millions of people reading your first novel).

Subject

The subject is the person or thing that your sentence is about. The key is to remember that all sentences have a subject and a verb – they go hand in hand. The subject is whoever or whatever is 'doing' the verb. For example, in the sentence,

'*Jack* sang a song,'
Jack is singing, so he is the subject.

Predicate

The predicate is the rest of the sentence – the part that isn't the subject:

'Jack *sang a song.*'
The predicate always includes the verb.

Object

The object is the person or thing that the verb is being done to. In the sentence above, the *song* is being sung by Jack, so the song is the object.

Clauses And Phrases

The sentence, 'Jack sang a song,' is short and simple, but if you add groups of words, called clauses and phrases, you'll give your readers more detail.

A clause is a group of words that includes a subject and a verb. A phrase is a group of words that doesn't include a subject and verb, and doesn't make sense on its own.

For example, in the sentence,
   'The boy sang a song while he grinned at his friends,'
there are two clauses. The first,
   'The boy sang a song,'
could be a sentence by itself. This is known as an independent clause. The second,
   'while he grinned at his friends,'
could not be a sentence by itself. This is known as a dependent clause because it relies on the first clause to make a complete sentence.

However, in the sentence,
   'The young boy tried to sing a cheerful song,'
the words, 'The young boy' make up one phrase, with a noun in it (the subject of the sentence – our hero, Jack). It is what is called a noun phrase. The words, 'tried to sing' are another phrase (a verb phrase this time). Lastly, the phrase, 'a cheerful song' is another noun phrase and it is also the object of the sentence. None of these three phrases makes any sense on its own.

UNUSUAL TERMS

Learn these terms and you'll soon be ready to impress.

Allegory

An allegory is a story with a hidden meaning. For instance, *Animal Farm*, a book by George Orwell, sounds as though it might be a simple tale about farm animals. In fact, it's about the communist government in Russia during the 1930s. Orwell used the animals, and their behaviour, to represent different kinds of people in the real world.

Cliché

Lots of sayings and expressions become dull if you hear them too often. When your teachers come out with an old saying such as, 'You must have ants in your pants,' when you are fidgeting, you can tell them they are using a cliché. (They might not appreciate it though.)

Diphthong

A diphthong is when you pronounce one vowel sound and slide into another by changing the position of your tongue in your mouth. It's not as complicated as it sounds though – when you say the word 'boil', for example, the sound you are making is a diphthong. Try saying the following words aloud, too: 'tail', 'feel', 'wear'. Listen to how the vowel sounds join as you move from one to the next in the same breath.

Oxymoron

An oxymoron is not an insult. Oxymorons combine two expressions or words that contradict each other. If you deliberately forget to tidy your room, for example, you may do so 'accidentally on purpose', causing your mother to complain that it's a 'fine mess' and to be so angry there is a 'deafening silence'.

Paradox

A paradox is something that seems impossible and yet may be true. If your parents make sure you do your homework, they may tell you they are 'being cruel to be kind'. It might appear impossible to be kind by being cruel, but they really mean that they're making you do something you'd rather not do, so that you get a good education.

Rhetorical Question

A rhetorical question is one that you don't expect anyone to answer. For instance, if you say, 'How should I know where your shoes are?' when a brother or sister has lost theirs, you wouldn't expect them to tell you exactly how they think you should know.

Tautology

Tautology means unnecessary repetition. For example, the expression 'free gift' is a tautology because the whole point of a gift is that it's free, so it's better just to say 'gift'.

SOUNDS LIKE ...

Homonyms

Some words have prefixes (at the beginning) and suffixes (at the end). In the word 'homonym', 'homo-' is the prefix, which comes from a Greek word meaning 'the same'. The suffix '-nym' comes from the Greek word for 'name', so homonyms give the same name to different meanings. For example, the word 'cross' has three homonyms: you can cross (travel over) a road, you can be cross (angry) and you can draw a cross (shape).

Homophones

The suffix '-phone' means 'sound'. Homophones are words that sound the same but are spelled differently. This sentence has three pairs of homophones:

The *band* was *banned* and so not *allowed* to play *aloud*, so you can't *hear* them *here*.

Synonyms

The prefix 'syn-' also means 'the same'. Synonyms are words with the same, or nearly the same, meaning. For instance, if you want to write about a great holiday, instead of using the word 'great' repeatedly, why not mention the 'lovely' weather or the 'brilliant' beach?

Antonyms

The prefix 'ant-' means 'opposed to', so an antonym has the opposite meaning. An antonym of 'good' is 'bad' and an antonym of 'wet' is 'dry'.

LET'S FIGURE THIS OUT

A 'figure of speech' is a way of using words for effect. There are all sorts of figures of speech you can use to create different effects with language. Here are some of them:

Metaphor And Simile

Metaphors and similes are easy to confuse as they are both ways of comparing things. Similes describe one thing as similar to another thing, usually using the words 'like' or 'as'. Your parents might say, 'You're as good as gold', or, 'You eat like a pig', for example. However, a metaphor says that a thing actually *is* something else – your parents might say, 'You're an angel', if you behave or, 'You're a little monster', if you don't, but you're not really an angel or a monster.

Alliteration

Alliteration is a group of words that begin with the same letter. For example, you could describe the 'wild, windy weather' or 'swirling, stormy sky'. It is often used in poetry as a writing device to add emphasis.

Assonance

Repetition of vowel sounds in words is called assonance –
it's also a technique that poets like to use to add dramatic
effect, as in the first line of Edgar Allen Poe's poem,
The Raven:

> 'Once upon a midnight dreary,
>   while I pondered weak and weary'

Here, the word 'weak' uses almost the same vowel sound
as the words 'dreary' and 'weary'.

Hyperbole

If you say that you're 'starving', your parents don't call an
ambulance, do they? What you really mean is that you are
hungry, but you are exaggerating for effect. This is called
hyperbole (which is pronounced 'hye-per-boh-lee').

Onomatopoeia

This strange word (pronounced 'on-uh-mat-oh-pee-ya')
describes the use of words that sound like a sound. For
instance, the 'hiss' of a hissing snake sounds like the noise a
snake makes. There are many words like this. For example,
water 'splashes', dropped pans 'clatter' and bells 'bong'.

Personification

Personification gives an object or animal qualities that
usually belong to people. If you write, 'The sun smiled
down on us,' you are using personification because the sun
doesn't really smile, people do.

LANGUAGES OF THE WORLD

There are thousands of languages in the world, but the best languages to learn depends upon where you live, where you might go on holiday and what your interests are. Here are a few ideas, with some useful words to start you off.

Arabic

Arabic is the official language of more than 15 countries, including Morocco and Saudi Arabia. It is written in a different alphabet to English, so the translations here represent their pronunciation.

Hello – *Ahlan wa sahlan*
Goodbye – *Salam*
Please – *Min fadlak*
Thank you – *Shukran*

Spanish

As well as being spoken in Spain and most of Central and South America, Spanish is also spoken by millions of people in the US. The pronunciation guide (in brackets) is based on Spanish as it is spoken in Spain, with the emphasized syllables in **bold**.

Hello – *Hola* (o–**la**)
Goodbye – *Adiós* (a-dee-**os**)
Please – *Por favour* (por **fa**-bor)
Thank you – *Gracias* (**grath**-i-as)

German

German is spoken in Germany, Austria and parts of Switzerland. It's from the same language family as English, so some words sound familiar and many words mean the same in English and German – 'hand', 'name' and 'warm', for instance – although they are pronounced slightly differently.

Hello – *Hallo* (ha-**lo**)
Goodbye – *Auf Wiedersehen* (owf **vee**-da-zayn)
Please – *Bitte* (bit-uh)
Thank you – *Danke* (dan-kuh)

French

French is an official language of more than 25 countries in the world including France, Belgium, Canada, Haiti and Mali.

Hello – *Bonjour* (bon-jor)
Goodbye – *Au revoir* (oh reh-**vwa**)
Please – *S'il vous plaît* (see-voo-play)
Thank you – *Merci* (mer-**see**)

English uses many French words and expressions such as 'rendezvous' (a meeting) and 'en route' (on the way).

Japanese

Japanese is written in symbols rather than letters. There are three different sets of symbols, called 'kanji', 'katakana' and 'hiragana'.

Hello – *Konnichiwa* (konni-chi-**wah**)
Goodbye – *Sayonara* (sigh-**yoh**-nah-rah)
Please – *Onegaishimasu* (on-eh-guy-she-mass-ou)
Thank you – *Arigato* (a-ri-**gah**-toh)

Japanese words such as 'kimono' and 'karate' are now used in everyday English .

CLASSICS STUFF

A DIP INTO THE CLASSICS

The subject of 'classics' is the study of the history, art and language of the ancient Greek and Roman civilizations.

Ancient Greece

The civilization of ancient Greece flourished between about 1,000 BCE and 300 BCE. The Greeks had ideas about science, art, philosophy (thinking about the meaning of stuff) and politics that are still valued today. They came up with the idea of 'democracy' – a political system in which ordinary people play a major role in governing themselves. It is the form of government that the majority of countries still use.

The Greeks were famous for their great philosophers. In the 5th century BCE, for example, a man named Socrates (sok-ra-teez) asked his students questions, such as 'What is right and wrong?', to help them think about the world around them. However, Socrates didn't leave anything written down, so Plato, one of his students, jotted it all down instead. Plato started 'The Academy', in Athens, a forerunner to today's universities. His most famous student, Aristotle, became a great scientist as well as a philosopher.

Greece was also home to many talented storytellers. According to legend, a blind poet named Homer (not to be confused with Homer Simpson!) was said to have composed two very long poems, the *Iliad* and the *Odyssey*. People told each other his stories and they passed down from one generation to the next. However, writers such as Sophocles (sof-o-kleez), Aeschylus (ee-ska-lus) and Euripides (you-rip-id-eez) wrote lots of great plays, many of which are still performed today.

Life wasn't all studying for the ancient Greeks. They also held huge sporting events. One of these took place in a city called Olympia every four years. Men from all over the Greek world took part in events such as the javelin, discus and chariot racing (women had their own competitions). Most sports were performed naked, as you can see here:

It was not until 1896 that the modern Olympic Games began (though people now prefer to get dressed first).

The Roman Empire

According to legend, Mars, the God of War, had two sons, Romulus and Remus, who were abandoned and cared for by a wolf. These brothers grew up to establish the great city of Rome in about 750 BCE.

Although this story is highly unlikely, Rome came to have immense power. Whenever the Romans conquered an area, their skilled craftsmen built towns with aqueducts (to bring water), bridges, bathhouses, theatres and temples. They also built roads so that their army could move around quickly. You can still visit many Roman buildings in places all over Europe, North Africa, Asia and the Middle East. One of the most famous sites is Pompeii, a town located in southern Italy. On 24th August CE 79, a volcanic eruption from nearby Mount Vesuvius destroyed the town and Pompeii was buried in falling ash. This preserved both the buildings and the town's people where they fell, until the 18th century when its ashy remains were uncovered.

Despite their advanced civilization, the Romans could be very cruel. At the Colosseum, an arena in Rome, thousands of people watched as gladiators (warriors) fought to the death, or as prisoners were thrown to lions.

For many years, Rome was ruled as a democracy, in a similar way to Greece. One of the men thought to have brought about the end of this democracy was Julius Caesar, a successful Roman general. He conquered many lands and, when he returned to Rome, made himself dictator for life. This meant that he was not elected by the people and had unlimited powers. It was short-lived, as he was assassinated soon afterwards, in 44 BCE, on the 'ides' of March (in the Roman calendar, the 15th of March, May, July and October and the 13th of every other month were all called the ides).

For the rest of its history, Rome was ruled by emperors who had control of a highly disciplined army. The army was divided into sections called legions, which each had around 4,800 soldiers, plus supporting horsemen and archers.

Some of these emperors were not very pleasant. Nero, for example, who reigned from CE 54 to CE 68, was said to have murdered his own mother, executed his first wife and may have murdered his second. His cruelty wasn't limited to his family – he was said to have had Christians burned to death at night to light up his garden. Eventually, the senate (the Roman government) had enough and sentenced Nero to death. Nero avoided execution by killing himself.

 ## ANCIENT LANGUAGES

Many people describe ancient Greek and Latin, the language of ancient Rome, as 'dead' languages. This is because no one has spoken them as everyday languages for a long time. However, they are still important today because thousands of words in modern languages come from Latin and Greek.

For example, in Latin, the word for 'moon' is *luna* – you'll spot it being used in English in words such as 'lunar' (a lunar cycle is the cycle of the moon) and 'lunacy' (another word for madness because people once thought that the moon affected people's behaviour). *Aqua*, the Latin for water, appears in 'aquatic' (aquatic creatures live in water). *Ignis*, or fire, can be seen in words such as 'ignite', which means to set alight.

In ancient Greek, *angelus* meant 'messenger', which is where the word 'angel' comes from, because angels are described as messengers from God. The word for an 'octopus' comes from *okto*, the Greek word meaning 'eight'. The link isn't always so obvious, though. For example, the word 'hippopotamus' comes from the Greek *hippos* (horse) and *potamos* (river), so a hippopotamus is a 'river horse'.

Ancient words can be used in combination to make new words, too. For example, the words *tele* and *phone* mean 'far away' and 'voice', so a telephone is just a 'far-away voice'.

The Greek Alphabet

Although the Romans wrote using pretty much the same letters as English, the Greek alphabet was (and still is) very different. You will probably come across some of these letters when you study maths and science, but here are all of them, in the correct order:

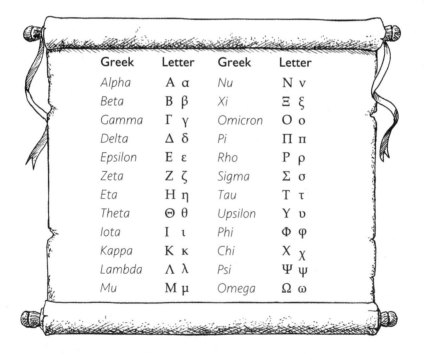

Greek	Letter	Greek	Letter
Alpha	A α	*Nu*	N ν
Beta	B β	*Xi*	Ξ ξ
Gamma	Γ γ	*Omicron*	O o
Delta	Δ δ	*Pi*	Π π
Epsilon	E ε	*Rho*	P ρ
Zeta	Z ζ	*Sigma*	Σ σ
Eta	H η	*Tau*	T τ
Theta	Θ θ	*Upsilon*	Y υ
Iota	I ι	*Phi*	Φ φ
Kappa	K κ	*Chi*	X χ
Lambda	Λ λ	*Psi*	Ψ ψ
Mu	M μ	*Omega*	Ω ω

Notice that the first two letters are *alpha* and *beta*, which are where the word 'alphabet' comes from when the two words are combined.

THE SEVEN WONDERS

There were many wonders in the ancient world, and those that the ancients regarded as the most amazing are known as the Seven Wonders of the Ancient World. Sadly only one is still standing today.

1. The Statue of Zeus at Olympia. The statue took a Greek sculptor, named Phidias, eight years to complete. It was nearly 12 metres tall and stood in Zeus's temple at Olympia. It showed him sitting on his throne, and was decorated with gold, precious stones and ivory.

VII Wonders Theme Park

2. The Temple of Artemis at Ephesus. This huge temple, in what is now Turkey, was decorated with beautiful works of art. It was so magnificent that Philon of Byzantium, who had seen all the other wonders, wrote that when he saw the temple, 'all these other wonders were put in the shade.'

3. The Colossus of Rhodes. The people of the Greek port of Rhodes defeated an invading army and celebrated by building a 32-metre-tall bronze and iron statue of the sun god, Helios. When it was destroyed by an earthquake less than 60 years after it was finished, the citizens of Rhodes decided not to rebuild it as they thought that the statue may have angered Helios.

4. The Mausoleum of Halicarnassus. This tomb in Turkey was built by Artemisia for her husband, King Mausolus, when he died. She sent for the best artists in the world to decorate it with statues and carvings. Artemisia died before building was complete and was placed next to her husband.

5. The Hanging Gardens of Babylon. The gardens, in what is now Iraq, were said to be full of exotic trees, plants and flowers, arranged on high platforms. It is said the gardens were built by King Nebuchadnezzar as a gift for his wife.

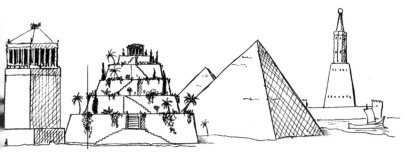

6. The Pyramids of Giza. The three pyramids were each built to hold the body of an Egyptian king (Khufu, Khafre and Menkaure). The Great Pyramid of Khufu needed 2,300,000 huge stone blocks and took tens of thousands of workers many years to complete. Despite being roughly 4,500 years old, the pyramids are the only wonder you can still see today.

7. The Pharos of Alexandria. The Pharos was a huge lighthouse, built to guide ships into the Egyptian port of Alexandria. There was a fire constantly burning at the top of a tower that was at least 115 metres tall, with a large mirror of polished metal to reflect the light across the sea.

MYTHOLOGICALLY SPEAKING

The ancient Greeks worshipped hundreds of gods and goddesses. They believed that the gods lived on Mount Olympus, which they thought linked Earth to Heaven. Later, the Romans often gave Greek gods Roman names and worshipped them, too. Gods and goddesses could stand for different things and really didn't behave very well. Here are just a few, followed by some stories about them:

Greek God	Roman God	Role
Zeus	Jupiter	Sky god and ruler of all the other gods – his weapon was a thunderbolt.
Hera	Juno	Zeus's wife, and goddess of marriage, known for being angry and jealous as Zeus often betrayed her.
Hades	Pluto	God of the underworld.
Apollo	Apollo	Son of Zeus and god of healing and music, as well as lots of other things.
Artemis	Diana	Goddess of hunting and wild animals, twin sister of Apollo.
Ares	Mars	God of war – in Greek stories he was thoughtlessly violent, but was much more likeable in Roman versions.
Aphrodite	Venus	Goddess of love and beauty.
Hermes	Mercury	The messenger of the gods with winged sandals, he was thought to bring luck to and protect travellers.
Athena	Minerva	Goddess of war and wisdom (and handicrafts). Her symbol was the owl.
Hephaestus	Vulcan	God of fire and craftsman for the gods who used volcanoes (which are named after him) to forge weapons.
Poseidon	Neptune	God of the sea.
Persephone	Proserpina	Daughter of Zeus and Demeter (goddess of the harvest).

Persephone

Lots of myths were told to help explain how the world worked. For example, the story of Persephone describes the changing of the seasons. She was the daughter of Zeus and Demeter. Hades, god of the underworld, wished to marry Persephone, but her mother wouldn't let him, so Hades kidnapped Persephone. Demeter was so angry that, as goddess of the harvest, she refused to let crops grow, threatening to starve the human race to death.

Zeus sent the messenger Hermes to force Hades to release Persephone – he agreed, but gave her a pomegranate before she left. Persephone was not allowed to eat food in the underworld, so after eating only one seed, she had to spend a third of every year in the underworld. Demeter would become so sad during this time each year that crops did not grow and winter came.

Daedalus And Icarus

Daedalus, who was an inventor and architect, was asked to build a labyrinth (or maze) for King Minos of Crete. As Daedalus knew how to escape the Labyrinth, he was not allowed to leave the island. To get away, he made a pair of wings for himself and his son, Icarus, by joining feathers together with wax. Icarus was thrilled. He flew higher and higher until he was too close to the sun. The heat melted the wax, causing him to plummet to his death in the sea below.

I TOLD YOU SO! YOU NEVER LISTEN TO ME.

Sisyphus

Sisyphus certainly knew how to annoy the gods. One day, he betrayed Zeus and was supposed to be punished with death. However, instead of dying, when Hades came to take him to the underworld, Sisyphus took Hades prisoner.

While Hades was trapped, no one in the world could die. Hades was rescued by Ares, and together they made sure that Sisyphus got to the underworld this time. However, Sisyphus was sneaky and escaped death again. This time Zeus sent Hermes to fetch him and Sisyphus was condemned to push a huge rock up a hill forever. As soon as he got near the top, the rock rolled back down to the bottom and Sisyphus had to begin pushing all over again.

Heracles

From an early age, Heracles, a warrior and half god, was harassed by Hera, Zeus's wife. She hated him because Zeus was his father. She even sent two snakes to try to kill him when he was a baby. However, young Heracles was so strong that he strangled them both.

Instead of killing him, Hera tormented Heracles and drove him so mad that he killed his own wife and children. The Oracle at Delphi told Heracles that, to make amends for the murders, he must serve King Eurystheus and perform any task set for him. With Hera's help, King Eurystheus came up with a series of what seemed to be impossible tasks, known as the 'Labours of Heracles' (see opposite).

Heracles was a true hero, however, and completed all the tasks. He continued to have adventures until he died, poisoned by the blood of a centaur (a creature that is half man and half horse). Here are the tasks Heracles was set:

1. To kill and skin the Nemean Lion.

2. To slay the nine-headed monster, Hydra.

3. To catch the sacred and swift-running Arcadian Hind (deer).

4. To capture the flesh-eating Erymanthian Boar.

5. To clean the overflowing cattle stables of King Augeas.

6. To defeat the man-eating Stymphalian Birds.

7. To capture the fire-breathing Cretan Bull.

8. To catch the Mares of King Diomedes – flesh-eating horses.

9. To bring Eurystheus the golden belt of Hippolyte, Queen of the fierce female Amazon warriors.

10. To steal the cattle of Geryon, the strongest man in the world.

11. To steal the golden apples of immortality from the Hesperides, daughters of the god Atlas.

12. To descend into the underworld and capture the many-headed guard dog, Cerberus.

HISTORY STUFF

BRITISH KINGS AND QUEENS

Here are Britain's kings and queens, with the dates of their reign, starting with Alfred the Great back in the 9th century when England was divided into several different kingdoms. Read more about the ones in **bold** on the following pages:

Alfred the Great	871-899	Henry V	1413-1422
Edward the Elder	899-924	Henry VI	1422-1461, 1470-1471
Athelstan	924-939	Edward IV	1461-1470, 1471-1483
Edmund the Magnificent	939-946	Edward V	1483
Eadred	946-955	Richard III Crookback	1483-1485
Eadwig (or Edwy) the Fair	955-959	Henry VII Tudor	1485-1509
Edgar the Peacemaker	959-975	**Henry VIII**	1509-1547
Edward the Martyr	975-978	Edward VI	1547-1553
Aethelred the Unready	978-1016	**Lady Jane Grey**	1553
Swein Forkbeard	1013	Mary I Tudor	1553-1558
Edmund Ironside	1016	Elizabeth I	1558-1603
Canute the Great	1016-1035	James I	1603-1625
Harold Harefoot	1035-1040	Charles I	1625-1649
Hardicanute	1040-1042	Oliver Cromwell *	1653-1658
Edward the Confessor	1042-1066	Richard Cromwell **	1658-1659
Harold II	1066	Charles II	1660-1685
William I the Conqueror		James II	1685-1688
	1066-1087	William III, Mary II †	1689-1702
William II 'Rufus'	1087-1100	Anne	1702-1714
Henry I Beauclerc	1100-1135	George I	1714-1727
Stephen	1135-1154	George II	1727-1760
Henry II Curtmantle	1154-1189	George III	1760-1820
Richard I the Lionheart	1189-1199	George IV	1820-1830
John Lackland	1199-1216	William IV	1830-1837
Henry III	1216-1272	**Victoria**	1837-1901
Edward I Longshanks	1272-1307	Edward VII	1901-1910
Edward II	1307-1327	George V	1910-1936
Edward III	1327-1377	Edward VIII	1936
Richard II	1377-1399	George VI	1936-1952
Henry IV Bolingbroke	1399-1413	Elizabeth II	from 1952

* Between 1649 and 1653, following the English Civil War, Britain had no head of state. Cromwell ruled England as Lord Protector from 1653 (see page 63).
** Oliver Cromwell's son ruled England briefly after his father died, until Charles II was invited to be king.
† Ruled jointly until Mary's death in 1694.

Alfred The Great

Alfred was King of an area in the southwest of England called Wessex. When Vikings from Scandinavia invaded, Alfred fled and legend says he hid with a peasant woman before returning to defeat the invaders. England was then divided into two areas – one ruled by Alfred, who was called 'King of the English' and one, known as the Danelaw, ruled by the Vikings. Alfred's son and grandson went on to gain control of even more land until England was finally united.

Canute The Great

Canute was a Viking warrior who became King of England through conquest. He was also King of Denmark and Norway, so was able to stop the Vikings attacking England. This made things much more peaceful. Legend says that Canute once had his throne put on the seashore, where he sat and commanded the incoming tide to halt – which, of course, it didn't. Some say he did it to prove to his subjects that kings were ordinary people and not gods.

William The Conqueror

William Duke of Normandy (in France) invaded England in 1066 and was crowned William I of England. He ruthlessly crushed uprisings and gave English lands to other Normans. The Bayeux Tapestry, a 70-metre-long embroidery, which dates from this time, describes the invasion in pictures.

Richard I

King Richard was believed to be so brave, he was known as 'the Lionheart'. He was king for 10 years, but only ever spent a few months in England. In 1190, he set off on an expedition called a Crusade (see page 59) to capture the holy city of Jerusalem from the Muslims, who were led by a man named Saladin. After fierce fighting, he made a truce with Saladin and returned to England. However, he set off again before long, this time to wage war with France where he was killed.

Henry VIII

Henry VIII wanted a son and, when he failed to have one with his first wife, Catherine of Aragon, he wished to have the marriage annulled (a kind of cancelling, rather than divorce). Britain was a Catholic country at that time and the Pope, head of the Catholic Church, refused. So Henry made himself head of the Church in England and married Anne Boleyn. However, when he grew tired of her, he had her head chopped off and married Jane Seymour next. After Jane died, he married and divorced

Anne of Cleves. He then married Catherine Howard, but had her beheaded so that he could marry Catherine Parr. She was lucky enough to outlive him.

Lady Jane Grey

Lady Jane's reign is perhaps the saddest in English history. The royal court was a place of scheming and plotting, and it suited a few powerful people to have Lady Jane made queen. Unfortunately, this didn't suit everybody and a rebellion broke out. The poor 15-year-old girl was queen for only nine days, before she was taken to the Tower of London and later beheaded.

Victoria

Victoria became queen at the age of 18 and remained on the throne for almost 64 years. Up until 2015, when Elizabeth II surpassed her, Queen Victoria had been Britain's longest-serving monarch. Her reign was a time of great scientific and technological advances. Perhaps the best proof of Britain's success during Victoria's reign was the Great Exhibition, held in 1851. It was designed to show off Britain's power, wealth and achievements to the world.

During Victoria's reign, Britain was at the height of its powers and had built a huge empire. In 1876, Victoria was also made Empress of India, when the British took full control of the country after several mutinies (rebellions) against their rule.

IN SEARCH OF CONQUEST

Throughout history, countries all over the world have looked to expand their lands by conquering other people's.

Conquerors And Invaders

The Crusades. In the 11th century, Muslim forces captured the holy city of Jerusalem. In response, the Pope launched a series of holy wars against them, known as the Crusades. These continued over the next 200 years. There was even a Children's Crusade where thousands of young children set out for Jerusalem. Arriving at the French port of Marseilles, they set sail for the Holy Land, only to be captured and sold into slavery.

Genghis Khan. In the 13th century, Genghis united the tribes of Mongolia, in east Asia. He led an army of fierce, nomadic tribesman on a violent trail of conquest through northern China, Russia and Eastern Europe. Each time Ghengis conquered a kingdom, the defeated soldiers joined him, so his army grew larger and larger.

North America. When Europeans settled in North America, they took land from the Native Americans who lived there already. This led to violent battles. One such battle is known as Custer's Last Stand. In June 1876, troops were sent to confront the Sioux and Cheyenne tribes near the Little Bighorn river, in South Dakota. The 7th Cavalry, led by George Armstrong Custer, tried to surround a large group of Sioux and Cheyenne warriors, but they were overwhelmed. Custer and more than 250 men were slain.

EXPLORING THE GLOBE

From the beginning of history, people have wondered what was over the next hill or across the ocean, and some people set off to find out.

A Few Great Explorers

Early Explorers. As early as the 4th century BCE, a Greek man named Pytheas, explored northwestern Europe. He may even have reached the Arctic Circle. In the 11th century, a Viking, Leif Erikson, reached America. Marco Polo, a Venetian explorer, arrived at the court of the great Kublai Khan, in China in 1266. His book, *Travels of Marco Polo*, made him the most famous explorer of all time.

Christopher Columbus. In 1492, an Italian named Christopher Columbus tried to reach Asia by sailing west around the world rather than east. Instead of reaching Asia, he discovered the 'New World' – Cuba, the Bahamas, Jamaica and Hispaniola (now Haiti and the Dominican Republic).

Cook and Livingstone. Englishman James Cook (later made a Captain) discovered New Zealand in 1769 and Australia a year later. In the 1850s, the Scottish explorer Doctor Livingstone became the first European to cross Africa. He found the Zambezi River in 1851 and, in 1855, was the first European to see Zambezi's Victoria Falls.

PRIME MINISTERS

In the United Kingdom, the leader of the political party in power is called the prime minister. Here is a list of every prime minister so far, with the dates of their time in office. Find out more about the prime ministers written in **bold** on the following page.

Sir Robert Walpole	1721-1742	Viscount Melbourne	1835-1841
Earl of Wilmington	1742-1743	Sir Robert Peel	1841-1846
Henry Pelham	1743-1754	Lord John Russell	
Duke of Newcastle	1754-1756	(later Earl Russell)	1846-1852
Duke of Devonshire	1756-1757	Earl of Derby	1852
Duke of Newcastle	1757-1762	Earl of Aberdeen	1852-1855
Earl of Bute	1762-1763	Viscount Palmerston	1855-1858
George Grenville	1763-1765	Earl of Derby	1858-1859
Marquess of Rockingham		Viscount Palmerston	1859-1865
	1765-1766	Earl Russell	1865-1866
William Pitt The Elder	1766-1768	Earl of Derby	1866-1868
Duke of Grafton	1768-1770	Benjamin Disraeli	1868
Lord North	1770-1782	**William Gladstone**	1868-1874
Marquess of Rockingham	1782	Benjamin Disraeli	1874-1880
Earl of Shelburne	1782-1783	William Gladstone	1880-1885
Duke of Portland	1783	Marquess of Salisbury	1885-1886
William Pitt The Younger		William Gladstone	1886
	1783-1801	Marquess of Salisbury	1886-1892
Henry Addington	1801-1804	William Gladstone	1892-1894
William Pitt The Younger		Earl of Rosebery	1894-1895
	1804-1806	Marquess of Salisbury	1895-1902
Lord Grenville	1806-1807	Arthur Balfour	1902-1905
Duke of Portland	1807-1809	Sir Henry Campbell-Bannerman	
Spencer Perceval	1809-1812		1905-1908
Earl of Liverpool	1812-1827	Herbert Asquith	1908-1916
George Canning	1827	David Lloyd George	1916-1922
Viscount Goderich	1827-1828	Andrew Bonar Law	1922-1923
Duke of Wellington	1828-1830	Stanley Baldwin	1923-1924
Earl Grey	1830-1834	Ramsey MacDonald	1924
Viscount Melbourne	1834	Stanley Baldwin	1924-1929
Sir Robert Peel	1834-1835	Ramsey MacDonald	1929-1935

Stanley Baldwin	1935-1937	Edward Heath	1970-1974
Neville Chamberlain	1937-1940	Harold Wilson	1974-1976
Winston Churchill	1940-1945	James Callaghan	1976-1979
Clement Attlee	1945-1951	Margaret Thatcher	1979-1990
Winston Churchill	1951-1955	John Major	1990-1997
Sir Anthony Eden	1955-1957	Tony Blair	1997-2007
Harold Macmillan	1957-1963	Gordon Brown	2007-2010
Alec Douglas-Home	1963-1964	David Cameron	2010-2016
Harold Wilson	1964-1970	Theresa May	from 2016

William Pitt The Younger

At the age of 24, Pitt became the youngest prime minister ever. Many people made fun of him because of his age, but he proved his critics wrong and led the United Kingdom through some difficult times.

Sir Robert Peel

Sir Robert did a lot to help children. He banned coal mine owners from forcing them to work underground and cut their hours of work in factories. He also set up the police force, which is why British police officers were nicknamed 'Bobbies' (because 'Robert' can be shortened to 'Bobby').

William Gladstone

Gladstone was prime minister four times, even holding the position in his 80s. He passed a law that made it easier for children to get an education and introduced the type of elections we have today. This means that people are able to vote without anyone knowing who they choose to vote for.

Winston Churchill

Churchill famously led Britain to victory in the Second World War. He made rousing speeches, inspiring the British people during these difficult years. He was knighted in 1953 and became Sir Winston Churchill.

TROUBLED TIMES

When groups within one country fight each other, it is called a civil war. In the case of one group overthrowing the government, it is known as a revolution.

Civil Wars And Revolutions

English Civil War. In 1642, war broke out between supporters of King Charles I and those who thought the country should be ruled by Parliament. The Royalists (on the side of Charles I) finally surrendered. The King escaped, but was captured and later beheaded. Four years after Charles's execution, a man named Oliver Cromwell ruled England with the title Lord Protector.

French Revolution. On 14th July 1789, the people of Paris stormed the Bastille prison and freed its prisoners. This began a revolution that led to the beheading of the French king, Louis XVI. Thousands were beheaded by guillotine during a period known as the Reign of Terror and France became a 'republic' (ruled by the people).

Russian Revolution. The First World War caused great poverty in Russia and, in 1917, a group of people called the Bolsheviks, led by a man named Lenin, rose against Tsar Nicholas II, the Russian ruler. They seized power and formed the Union of Soviet Socialist Republics, which they intended to be run by ordinary working people. In reality, however, life remained hard and the Russian people had little freedom.

IN TIMES OF WAR

As well as fighting between themselves, many countries have fallen out with one another, too.

Some Rather Important Wars

The Napoleonic Wars. Napoleon Bonaparte led France into a series of battles against its European neighbours until France dominated Europe. However, in 1812, Napoleon invaded Russia. The harsh Russian winter forced him to retreat and he lost most of his army. Napoleon was exiled in 1814, but returned to power only to be defeated at the Battle of Waterloo. In 1815, he was exiled again.

The First World War. Beginning in 1914, with Germany and Austria fighting Britain, France and Russia, this war spread from Europe to involve countries across the world. It was the first modern war – with machine guns, poison gas, tanks and planes. Hundreds of thousands of men were killed in horrific battles, including those at the Somme and Verdun, in France, and at Passchendaele and Ypres, in Belgium. In 1918, Germany surrendered.

The Second World War. The rise of the dictator Adolf Hitler and the Nazis (an extreme political party) led Germany into war again. In 1939, Hitler invaded Poland, so Britain and France declared war on Germany. Many more countries became involved, including the USA and Japan before the war ended in 1945. The Second World War is known for two especially terrible events. During the war, six million Jews were murdered by the Nazis in what is known as the Holocaust. In 1945, two atomic bombs were dropped on cities in Japan causing great destruction (see page 69).

ALL THE US PRESIDENTS

There have been 43 presidents since the first, George Washington, was elected in February 1789. However, Grover Cleveland was both the 22ⁿᵈ and 24ᵗʰ president – the only one to have served two separate terms in office with another president in between. Below is a list of every president of the United States so far, with the dates of their time spent in office. You will find more detail on the presidents whose names are written in **bold** on the next few pages.

The Great Seal of the United States

1	**George Washington**	1789-1797	23	Benjamin Harrison	1889-1893
2	John Adams	1797-1801	24	Grover Cleveland	1893-1897
3	**Thomas Jefferson**	1801-1809	25	William McKinley **	1897-1901
4	James Madison	1809-1817	26	Theodore Roosevelt	1901-1909
5	James Monroe	1817-1825	27	William H. Taft	1909-1913
6	John Quincy Adams	1825-1829	28	**Woodrow Wilson**	1913-1921
7	Andrew Jackson	1829-1837	29	Warren G. Harding	1921-1923
8	Martin Van Buren	1837-1841	30	Calvin Coolidge	1923-1929
9	William Henry Harrison *	1841	31	Herbert C. Hoover	1929-1933
10	John Tyler	1841-1845	32	**Franklin D. Roosevelt** *	1933-1945
11	James K. Polk	1845-1849	33	Harry S. Truman	1945-1953
12	Zachary Taylor	1849-1850	34	Dwight D. Eisenhower	1953-1961
13	Millard Fillmore	1850-1853	35	**John F. Kennedy** **	1961-1963
14	Franklin Pierce	1853-1857	36	Lyndon B. Johnson	1963-1969
15	James Buchanan	1857-1861	37	**Richard Nixon**	1969-1974
16	**Abraham Lincoln** **	1861-1865	38	Gerald Ford	1974-1977
17	Andrew Johnson	1865-1869	39	Jimmy Carter	1977-1981
18	Ulysses S. Grant	1869-1877	40	Ronald Reagan	1981-1989
19	Rutherford B. Hayes	1877-1881	41	George H. W. Bush	1989-1993
20	James A. Garfield **	1881	42	Bill Clinton	1993-2001
21	Chester A. Arthur	1881-1885	43	George W. Bush	2001-2009
22	Grover Cleveland	1885-1889	44	**Barack Obama**	2009-2016

* Died in office ** Assassinated

George Washington

Washington was commander-in-chief of the forces rebelling against British rule in the 1770s – known as the American Revolution. He later became leader of the Constitutional Convention – an organization which decided how America should be run. He was elected as the first president of the United States. After serving two four-year terms, he chose not to stay on. This began the tradition that no president may spend more than eight years in office. The only exception to this is Franklin D. Roosevelt (see opposite).

Thomas Jefferson

Jefferson wrote much of the US Declaration of Independence, which states why the first 13 states split from British rule. One of his most recognizable lines says that 'all men are created equal' and that their rights should include 'life, liberty and the pursuit of happiness'. Congress approved the declaration on 4th July 1776, which is still celebrated as Independence Day. The American Revolution was eventually won seven years later.

Abraham Lincoln

When Lincoln was elected, seven pro-slavery Southern states who opposed him left the Union (of states) before his inauguration (when the President is sworn into office). Civil war broke out and four more states joined the South, forming the Confederate States of America. In 1862, Lincoln signed the Emancipation Proclamation (an official announcement, freeing slaves), which declared it illegal for anyone in the Confederate States to own slaves. Then, in 1863, Lincoln gave one of the shortest and most famous speeches of all time: the Gettysburg Address. This reminded people that their efforts in the war were for 'government

of the people, by the people, for the people'. Lincoln led the North to victory in 1865, but just five days after the war ended, a supporter of slavery named John Wilkes Booth shot and killed him. Slavery was officially abolished for the whole country later that year, with the 13th Amendment to the US constitution.

Woodrow Wilson

Wilson led America through the First World War and, at the end of the war, supported the League of Nations. This was an organization set up to encourage countries to co-operate with each other. He was awarded the Nobel Peace Prize for his work. Wilson also passed a number of important laws while in office, including banning child labour and giving women the right to vote.

Franklin D. Roosevelt

Franklin Delano Roosevelt (known as FDR for short) is the only president elected to office four times. He led the USA through some very difficult years. During a period called the Great Depression, when millions of Americans lost their jobs and suffered terrible poverty, Roosevelt introduced the 'New Deal', a programme to help tackle poor conditions. It helped businesses and those who had lost their jobs. After the Japanese bombed Pearl Harbour in 1941, Roosevelt led America through the Second World War, but he suffered from ill health towards the end of the war and died on 12th April 1945.

John F. Kennedy

At the age of just 43, Kennedy was America's youngest ever president. During his brief time in office, he pledged that the US would send a man to the moon by the end of the 1960s (which they did in 1969). In October 1962, he dealt with an incident called the Cuban Missile Crisis, when the world came close to nuclear war (see page 70). Kennedy was very popular. However, on 22nd November 1963, he was shot by a man named Lee Harvey Oswald while riding through Dallas, Texas, in an open-topped car.

Richard Nixon

Nixon was the first American president to resign. He was involved in the 'Watergate Scandal', in which five men were hired by Nixon's own political party to burgle their opponent's headquarters in the Watergate building, in Washington D.C. Things got worse when Nixon tried to cover up the scandal, so he resigned.

Barack Obama

Obama was the first black person to be elected as US president. He faced many challenges, including tackling the most serious financial crisis in decades, following the collapse of world financial markets in 2008. People were also hopeful that he would be able to find a solution to America's military involvement in Afghanistan and Iraq.

CLASSIFIED

Two of the most secret operations in history took place during the Second World War.

Top Secret

Station X. During the Second World War, Hitler's Germany had a code-making machine named Enigma. The chance of anyone cracking its codes were one in 150 million million million. A group of some of the brainiest people in Britain, gathered at 'Station X', an English stately home called Bletchley Park, where they worked day and night to break the codes. Their work was vital in helping the allies (Britain, the US, the Soviet Union and other countries) and meant that they could identify enemy plans in advance. Although thousands of people worked at Station X, not one person gave away its secrets. It wasn't until many years later that the importance of Bletchley Park became known.

The Manhattan Project. In 1939, the famous scientist Albert Einstein wrote to President Roosevelt about the importance of atomic research. In 1941, Roosevelt ordered the research to begin. It is known as the Manhattan Project because a lot of the first research was done at Columbia University, in Manhattan. A scientist named Robert Oppenheimer was later put in charge of the main laboratory, which was codenamed Project Y.

The atomic bomb was developed and two were dropped on the Japanese cities of Nagasaki and Hiroshima, in August 1945. This dealt the deciding blow for the US against Japan in Second World War. The Japanese surrendered, ending the war. Both cities were destroyed and over 200,000 people had died by the end of that year.

HOW COLD IS A COLD WAR?

In 1946, Winston Churchill spoke of an 'iron curtain' falling across Europe. He was referring to what eventually became known as the Cold War.

At the end of the Second World War, the victorious allied countries split into opposing sides. In Eastern Europe, Russia and 14 other communist states made up the Soviet Union. Western Europe, Britain and the US were known as 'the West' and in 1949, they created the North Atlantic Treaty Organization – known as 'NATO'. The Soviets placed pro-Soviet governments in power in Eastern Europe and in 1955 they formed a military alliance with these countries, which became known as the Warsaw Pact. They agreed to unite to defend themselves against the West.

East and West never actually declared war on each other, but both sides had enough nuclear weapons to destroy the world. There was a great deal of tension for many years. In 1962, when the Soviets placed missiles in Cuba, close to the USA, the world was on the brink of war for almost two weeks, before the Soviets agreed to withdraw the missiles.

In the 1980s, Mikhail Gorbachev, the president of the Soviet Union, introduced reforms. Eastern Europe began to break free from Soviet control. An event that particularly signalled the end of the Cold War was the destruction of the Berlin Wall – a wall built around West Berlin to separate it from communist East Berlin. For nearly 30 years, the wall stood as the symbol of the 'iron curtain', dividing East from West.

GEOGRAPHY STUFF

COUNTRIES, CONTINENTS AND CAPITAL CITIES

You'll already know that the world is divided into separate areas, called countries. But did you know that the number, size and shape of these areas haven't always been the same? The borders between countries have often been decided through war or political upheaval. A change in government may mean that two countries become a single country – for example, East and West Germany became just Germany in 1990. Or it can mean that one country is divided into smaller countries – Slovakia and the Czech Republic used to be just Czechoslovakia, for example.

Each country has a capital city – usually the largest city in the country – where the government meets to conduct official business. Exceptions to this rule include Tanzania, where the official capital has been Dodoma since 1996, but much of the government still meets in Dar es Salaam, the former capital.

Here is a list of all the countries of the world and their capital cities, divided by continent. The island countries of the Caribbean and those countries in Central America (the thin piece of land linking North and South America) have been listed separately to make them easier to find on a map – in fact, they belong with North America.

Africa

Country	Capital	Country	Capital
Algeria	Algiers	Lesotho	Maseru
Angola	Luanda	Liberia	Monrovia
Benin	Porto-Novo	Libya	Tripoli
Botswana	Gaborone	Madagascar	Antananarivo
Burkina Faso	Ouagadougou	Malawi	Lilongwe
Burundi	Bujumbura	Mali	Bamako
Cameroon	Yaoundé	Mauritania	Nouakchott
Cape Verde	Praia	Mauritius	Port Louis
Central African		Morocco	Rabat
Republic	Bangui	Mozambique	Maputo
Chad	N'Djamena	Namibia	Windhoek
Comoros	Moroni	Niger	Niamey
Congo (officially Republic		Nigeria	Abuja
of the Congo)	Brazzaville	Rwanda	Kigali
Congo		São Tomé	
(Democratic Republic		and Príncipe	São Tomé
of the Congo)	Kinshasa	Senegal	Dakar
Côte D'Ivoire		Seychelles	Victoria
(formerly	Yamoussoukro *	Sierra Leone	Freetown
Ivory Coast)	Abidjan **	Somalia	Mogadishu
Djibouti	Djibouti	South Africa	Pretoria †
Egypt	Cairo		Bloemfontain ††
Equatorial			Cape Town †††
Guinea	Malabo	Sudan	Khartoum
Eritrea	Asmara	Swaziland	Mbabane
Ethiopia	Addis Ababa	Tanzania	Dodoma ‡
Gabon	Libreville		Dar es Salaam ‡‡
Gambia, The	Banjul	Togo	Lomé
Ghana	Accra	Tunisia	Tunis
Guinea	Conakry	Uganda	Kampala
Guinea-Bissau	Bissau	Zambia	Lusaka
Kenya	Nairobi	Zimbabwe	Harare

* Official capital
** 'De facto' capital, meaning the unofficial centre of government

† Executive capital, where the laws are carried out
†† Judicial capital, where the country's judges sit and trials are held
††† Legislative capital, where laws are made

‡ Official capital ‡‡ Former capital, where parts of the government are still located

Asia

Country	Capital	Country	Capital
Afghanistan	Kabul	Maldives	Male
Armenia	Yerevan	Mongolia	Ulaanbaatar
Azerbaijan	Baku	Myanmar	
Bahrain	Manama	(formerly	
Bangladesh	Dhaka	Burma)	Nay Pyi Taw
Bhutan	Thimphu	Nepal	Kathmandu
Brunei	Bandar Seri	North Korea	Pyongyang
	Begawan	Oman	Muscat
Cambodia	Phnom Penh	Pakistan	Islamabad
China	Beijing	Philippines	Manila
East Timor		Qatar	Doha
(officially Democratic		Russia (Russian	Moscow
Republic of		Federation)	(also Europe)
Timor-Leste)	Dili	Saudi Arabia	Riyadh
Georgia	Tbilisi	Singapore	Singapore
India	New Delhi	South Korea	Seoul
Indonesia	Jakarta	Sri Lanka	Colombo †
Iran	Tehran		Sri Jayawar-
Iraq	Baghdad		denepura ††
Israel	Jerusalem	Syria	Damascus
Japan	Tokyo	Taiwan	Taipei
Jordan	Amman	Tajikistan	Dushanbe
Kazakhstan	Astana	Thailand	Bangkok
Korea, *see*		Turkey	Ankara
North Korea *and*			(also Europe)
South Korea		Turkmenistan	Ashgabat
Kuwait	Kuwait City	United Arab	
Kyrgyzstan	Bishkek	Emirates	Abu Dhabi
Laos	Vientiane	Uzbekistan	Tashkent
Lebanon	Beirut	Vietnam	Hanoi
Malaysia	Kuala Lumpur	Yemen	Sanaa

† Executive capital, where the laws are carried out
†† Legislative and judicial capital, where laws are made, the country's judges sit and trials are held

Europe

Country	Capital	Country	Capital
Albania	*Tirana*	Lithuania	*Vilnius*
Andorra	*Andorra la Vella*	Luxembourg	*Luxembourg*
Austria	*Vienna*	Macedonia	*Skopje*
Belarus	*Minsk*	Malta	*Valletta*
Belgium	*Brussels*	Moldova	*Chisinau*
Bosnia and		Monaco	*Monaco*
Herzegovina	*Sarajevo*	Montenegro	*Podgorica*
Bulgaria	*Sofia*	Netherlands	*Amsterdam ****
Croatia	*Zagreb*		*The Hague *****
Cyprus	*Nicosia*	Norway	*Oslo*
Czech Republic	*Prague*	Poland	*Warsaw*
Denmark	*Copenhagen*	Portugal	*Lisbon*
Estonia	*Tallinn*	Romania	*Bucharest*
Finland	*Helsinki*	Russia (Russian	*Moscow*
France	*Paris*	Federation)	*(also Asia)*
Germany	*Berlin*	San Marino	*San Marino*
Greece	*Athens*	Serbia	*Belgrade*
Hungary	*Budapest*	Slovakia	*Bratislava*
Iceland	*Reykjavik*	Slovenia	*Ljubljana*
Ireland	*Dublin*	Spain	*Madrid*
Italy	*Rome*	Sweden	*Stockholm*
Kosovo	*Pristina*	Switzerland	*Bern*
(declared itself independent, 2008)		Turkey	*Ankara (also Asia)*
		Ukraine	*Kiev*
Latvia	*Riga*	United Kingdom	*London*
Liechtenstein	*Vaduz*	Vatican City	*Vatican City*

Oceania

Country	Capital	Country	Capital
Australia	*Canberra*	Palau	*Melekeok*
Fiji	*Suva*	Papua	
Kiribati	*Bairiki*	New Guinea	*Port Moresby*
Marshall Islands	*Majuro*	Samoa	*Apia*
Micronesia (Federated States		Solomon Islands	*Honiara*
of Micronesia)	*Palikir*	Tonga	*Nuku'alofa*
Nauru	*Yaren*	Tuvalu	*Funafuti*
New Zealand	*Wellington*	Vanuatu	*Port Vila*

* Official capital, where the laws are carried out
** The city from which the country is governed

Central America And
The Caribbean

Country	Capital	Country	Capital
Antigua		Haiti	Port-au-Prince
and Barbuda	St John's	Honduras	Tegucigalpa
Bahamas, The	Nassau	Jamaica	Kingston
Barbados	Bridgetown	Nicaragua	Managua
Belize	Belmopan	Panama	Panama City
Costa Rica	San José	Saint Kitts	
Cuba	Havana	and Nevis	Basseterre
Dominica	Roseau	Saint Lucia	Castries
Dominican		Saint Vincent and	
Republic	Santo Domingo	the Grenadines	Kingstown
El Salvador	San Salvador	Trinidad	
Grenada	Saint George's	and Tobago	Port of Spain
Guatemala	Guatemala City		

North America

Canada	Ottawa	United States	
Mexico	Mexico City	of America	Washington D.C.

South America

Argentina	Buenos Aires	Guyana	Georgetown
Bolivia	La Paz †	Paraguay	Asunción
	Sucre ††	Peru	Lima
Brazil	Brasilia	Suriname	Paramaribo
Chile	Santiago	Uruguay	Montevideo
Colombia	Bogotá	Venezuela	Caracas
Ecuador	Quito		

† Administrative capital, where the main government is run
†† Judicial capital, where the country's judges sit and trials are held

THE UNITED STATES
OF AMERICA

The 50 states that make up the United States of America (the USA) today, are listed below. More states were created as the USA bought or conquered North American land that had previously been claimed by other people or nations. Alaska and Hawaii became the 49th and 50th states in 1959.

State	Capital	State	Capital
Alabama	Montgomery	Montana	Helena
Alaska	Juneau	Nebraska	Lincoln
Arizona	Phoenix	Nevada	Carson City
Arkansas	Little Rock	New Hampshire *	Concord
California	Sacramento	New Jersey *	Trenton
Colorado	Denver	New Mexico	Santa Fe
Connecticut *	Hartford	New York *	Albany
Delaware *	Dover	North Carolina *	Raleigh
Florida	Tallahassee	North Dakota	Bismarck
Georgia *	Atlanta	Ohio	Columbus
Hawaii	Honolulu	Oklahoma	Oklahoma City
Idaho	Boise	Oregon	Salem
Illinois	Springfield	Pennsylvania *	Harrisburg
Indiana	Indianapolis	Rhode Island *	Providence
Iowa	Des Moines	South Carolina *	Columbia
Kansas	Topeka	South Dakota	Pierre
Kentucky	Frankfort	Tennessee	Nashville
Louisiana	Baton Rouge	Texas	Austin
Maine	Augusta	Utah	Salt Lake City
Maryland *	Annapolis	Vermont	Montpelier
Massachusetts *	Boston	Virginia *	Richmond
Michigan	Lansing	Washington	Olympia
Minnesota	St Paul	West Virginia	Charleston
Mississippi	Jackson	Wisconsin	Madison
Missouri	Jefferson City	Wyoming	Cheyenne

* The 13 colonies along the east coast of the North American continent, where Europeans first settled in the 16th century

 TALLEST, LARGEST, LONGEST

No one is very interested in the world's tiniest mountain, smallest sea or shortest river, so here are the tallest mountains, largest oceans, and longest rivers instead.

Record-breaking World

Mountains. The tallest mountains in the world are all in an area called the Himalayas, in Asia. There are several measuring over 8,000 metres. These include Everest at 8,848 metres, K2 at 8,611 metres and Kanchenjunga at 8,598 metres tall.

Outside Asia, the tallest mountain is Aconcagua, in Argentina, which is 6,959 metres high. The USA's tallest is Mount McKinley in Alaska, at 6,194 metres, while in Africa, Kilimanjaro, in Kenya, tops the charts at 5,895 metres. Mont Blanc, which straddles the borders of France and Italy, is the tallest mountain in Europe at 4,807 metres.

Mauna Kea, a dormant (resting) volcano in the Hawaiian Islands, deserves a mention, too. Measuring 10,200 metres from base to top, it's taller than Everest, but only 4,205 metres of that is above the surface of the sea. The UK's tallest mountain, Ben Nevis in Scotland, is just 1,343 metres high.

Oceans. All oceans are connected, so in a way there is just one big ocean –

sometimes called the World Ocean. This is divided into the Pacific at 165.5 million square kilometres (or km²), the Atlantic at 81.5 million km², the Indian at 73.5 million km² and the Arctic at 14.1 million km².

Seas. Areas of water separating two land masses, often called seas, are also part of one of the main oceans. Some inland salt-water lakes are called seas too, but aren't really.

The largest sea in the world is the South China Sea at 3 million km². It lies between mainland Asia and the islands of the Philippines and is part of the Pacific Ocean. Next largest is the Caribbean at 2.8 million km², which is east of Central America and part of the Atlantic Ocean. The Mediterranean Sea, measuring 2.5 million km², is also part of the Atlantic, and lies between southern Europe and North Africa. The Bering Sea, at 2.3 million km², sits between Alaska and Russia and is part of the Pacific, and the Gulf of Mexico at 1.5 million km², separates eastern USA and Mexico and is part of the Atlantic (and is a sea).

Rivers. The Nile and the Amazon have been fighting for the title of 'the world's longest river' for years, but measuring a river isn't easy. Deciding where the sea stops and the river starts is one thing, then finding the river's true source (where it rises from the ground) is another. The five longest rivers, as their lengths currently stand, are the Nile in Egypt, which is 6,650 kilometres long, the Amazon in Brazil, at 6,450 kilometres, the Yangtze in China, at 6,380 kilometres, the Mississippi–Missouri in the USA, at 6,020 kilometres and Yenisey–Angara in Russia, at 5,550 kilometres.

The UK's longest river, at a measly 354 kilometres, is the Severn, with the Thames hot on its heels at 346 kilometres.

HOW LAND IS SHAPED
AND CHANGED

Mountains, oceans and rivers are constantly changing, by tiny amounts, but over the 4.6 billion years of the planet's life so far, it adds up to rather a lot. Here's how it changes:

Erosion

Land is worn away by the action of wind and water, which can even change the shape of coastlines. The land doesn't just vanish though, it gets moved elsewhere. For example, a fast-flowing river picks up gravel from the riverbed, carries it along, and deposits it again where the water slows down.

Glaciers

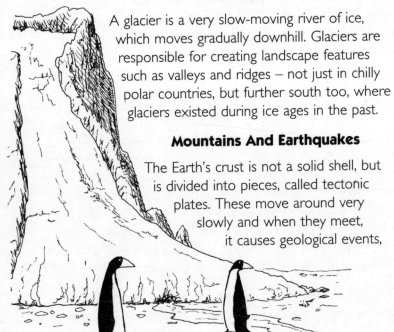

A glacier is a very slow-moving river of ice, which moves gradually downhill. Glaciers are responsible for creating landscape features such as valleys and ridges — not just in chilly polar countries, but further south too, where glaciers existed during ice ages in the past.

Mountains And Earthquakes

The Earth's crust is not a solid shell, but is divided into pieces, called tectonic plates. These move around very slowly and when they meet, it causes geological events, such as earthquakes, to take place. Many mountain ranges are the result of two plates colliding and pushing the land upwards. Everest, in the Himalayas, gets 6.1 centimetres taller each year as two plates push together. Earthquakes occur along boundaries between plates.

Volcanoes

The inside of the planet is far less pleasant than the surface because it is made of extremely hot melted rock called magma. A volcano is a point where a hole in the Earth's surface goes to an underground chamber full of magma. They are usually found along the edges of tectonic plates. Most are tall with craters (holes) in the centre. When an eruption occurs, ash and magma escape from the hole and can cause great destruction. The steep sides of a volcano are made of this ash and magma from previous eruptions.

Did You Know?

Magma hardens into stone as it cools and can make new land. For instance, Hawaii is a group of islands formed by underwater volcanoes erupting.

THE WATER CYCLE

Earth is the only place that scientists currently know of in the solar system where liquid water exists. It is continually recycled in a process called the water cycle, shown below:

3. As clouds rise, the vapour cools and condenses (into liquid water).

2. Water vapour collects in the sky, forming clouds.

4. This water falls back down to Earth as rain, snow or hail.

1. In the sun's heat, water evaporates (turns into vapour).

5. The water drains into lakes and seas via rivers.

Droughts

The quantity of water on Earth doesn't change, so it can be difficult to understand why many places don't have enough. In some countries, weather patterns (known as droughts) mean that very little rain falls for long periods of time. This can mean that there is not enough safe fresh water in those areas for people and animals to drink. Often, crops fail to grow, which leads to a shortage of food. Making sure that any available water is safe and doesn't contain disease-causing organisms is expensive and difficult.

WEATHER AND CLIMATE

Many people enjoy nothing more than discussing the weather, so next time someone complains about the rain, explain to them how weather systems work.

Wind, Rain And Wild Weather

Weather Patterns. Where rain or snow falls depends on the way air moves around above the Earth, which in turn depends on the sun warming the air.

Warm air tends to rise. This creates low pressure because the air is pressing down less against the Earth. Clouds form as the water vapour in the air cools and condenses into liquid water. Cooling air sinks, which creates high pressure and fewer clouds. Air tends to try to move from areas of high pressure to areas of low pressure, forming winds. Wind can carry clouds around and cause them to rain far away from where they were formed. The shape of the land affects the speed and direction of winds, and different winds can affect each other.

All of these factors produce the weather, but the process is very complex and chaotic, which is why forecasters are often wrong when they try to predict what might happen more than a few days in advance.

Climate Zones. Chaotic though the weather may be, you can be reasonably confident that you'll be warmer in Spain in July than you will in Moscow in January. The Earth is tilted on its axis (the vertical line through its centre around which it spins), so parts of it get more sunshine than others at different times of year. This produces seasons. If the planet didn't have this tilt, there would be no seasons anywhere.

At the North and South Poles, there are basically two seasons each year – a summer of 24-hour daylight when the pole faces the sun, and a winter of 24-hour night when it doesn't, with a very quick changeover. Few plants grow there, and most animals visit only in summer, leaving before winter begins. These areas are called the 'Polar' zones.

As you move away from the poles, summer days and winter nights get shorter and the changes between summer and winter get long enough to be called seasons in their own right: spring and autumn. Plants tend to grow more in spring and summer to make the most of sunlight. Countries with four distinct seasons are found in the 'Temperate' zones.

At the equator (the widest part of the Earth between the poles), there is no obvious spring, summer, autumn or winter. Instead, countries here have a rainy season and a dry season. They are in the 'Tropical' zone. Plants and animals often grow and reproduce throughout the year.

Extreme Weather. When areas of low-pressure air form in the middle of high-pressure air, there will often be storms. In heavy rainstorms, electricity is discharged from cloud to cloud or between the land and a cloud, producing lightning. The heat of the lightning passing through the air produces the sound of thunder. The time that passes between seeing the flash and hearing the rumble tells you how close the lightning is – every second equals roughly three kilometres.

Tornadoes. Tornadoes, caused by spinning funnels of air during thunderstorms, descend to the ground from large clouds. They suck up loose bits and pieces from the ground – these can even include cars and people if a tornado is large enough. Tornados over the sea can result in one of the rarest of all weather phenomenons: raining fish!

HUMAN IMPACT

Humans have lived on Earth for a relatively short time, but have made some noticeable changes to how things work. Here are some of the ways people have changed the planet:

• On the island of Madagascar, so many trees have been removed to make space for crops that hundreds of tonnes of soil have been washed away. So much soil, washed down from the hills, built up in the river basin that a port had to be moved to prevent ships running aground.

• Cattle and other animals bred for meat add to climate change with the gases in their burps and farts (no, really!).

• Some of the rubbish that humans throw away collects together in the ocean. The 'Great Pacific Garbage Patch', for example, is in fact two huge islands of floating plastic in the eastern and western Pacific Ocean. Together they measure several million square kilometres.

Did You Know?

Many materials that are used to package food take a huge amount of time to decompose (rot back into the ground). An aluminium fizzy drink can, for example, will still be around 100 years from now unless it is recycled. A plastic bag could take up to 1,000 years to decompose.

GEOLOGICAL TIME, IN BRIEF

Scientists believe the Earth was formed 4.6 billion years ago, but geological time is measured from 600 million years ago, with the start of the Palaeozoic era (geological time is divided into eras, then periods, then epochs). This was when the first multicellular (made of more than one cell) plants and animals first appeared, followed by the first primitive arthropods (animals such as insects, with jointed legs) and chordates (animals with spinal cords). At the end of this era, about 95% of all marine species became extinct, although a larger proportion of plants and animals on land survived – no one knows why for sure.

The Mesozoic era began 250 million years ago. Chordate animals became established on land and dinosaurs soon dominated the scene. Mammals and birds also appeared,

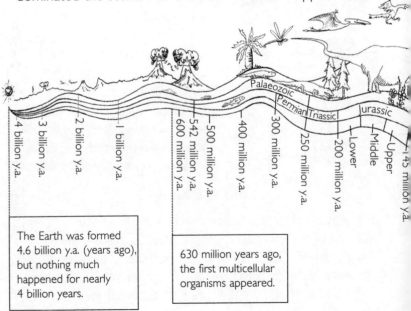

The Earth was formed 4.6 billion y.a. (years ago), but nothing much happened for nearly 4 billion years.

630 million years ago, the first multicellular organisms appeared.

descended from two separate kinds of reptiles. This era is divided into three periods – the Triassic, Jurassic and Cretaceous. At the end of this era, another mass extinction occurred (perhaps caused by a catastrophe such as a massive asteroid strike or huge volcanic eruptions). It wiped out a large proportion of life on the planet, including the dinosaurs, but that did mean there was more room for other mammals to thrive.

The Cenozoic era began 65 million years ago (the planet is still in it now). Mammals took over from dinosaurs and many new species evolved, including humans, who were first around some 200,000 years ago. There have been seven epochs in this era. The current epoch is the Holocene, but many scientists say that a new epoch should be recognized – the Anthropocene – dating from around the year 1800 CE when human impact on the Earth can be noticed.

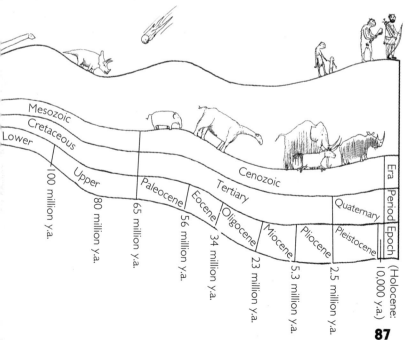

Mesozoic

Cretaceous

Lower

Upper

100 million y.a.

80 million y.a.

65 million y.a.

Paleocene

56 million y.a.

Eocene

34 million y.a.

Oligocene

Tertiary

Cenozoic

23 million y.a.

Miocene

5.3 million y.a.

Pliocene

2.5 million y.a.

Quaternary

Pleistocene

Era

Period

Epoch

(Holocene: 10,000 y.a.)

MATHS STUFF

WHAT'S IN A NUMBER?

Mathematics is very useful stuff. It's perfect for working out whether you're rich, for doing science and for keeping computers running. It isn't just a useful tool either; it's a whole world full of amazing and mysterious things.

When In Rome

For centuries, Roman numerals were widely used for counting and mathematics. They are written using the letters I (one), V (five), X (ten), L (fifty), C (a hundred), D (five hundred) and M (a thousand). The order the letters are written in tells you what the number is. For example, if you place a lower numeral in front of a larger numeral it reduces the value of the larger numeral – so 'CM' is 900. If you place a lower numeral after a larger numeral it raises the value of the larger numeral – so 'XV' is 15. Just to write '1915', you'd need to write out 'MCMXV'. Imagine trying to calculate a really complicated maths problem!

Number Symbols

The numbers that we use now – 1, 2, 3, 4, 5, 6, 7, 8 and 9 – are called Hindu-Arabic numerals. These symbols developed in India and the surrounding area over several hundred years. Traders going between North Africa and Spain then helped them spread to Europe, and when translations of mathematical writings became available, even more people learned about them. The invention of the printing press in the mid-15th century meant that the symbols became familiar to many more people, and eventually the Hindu-Arabic numerals took over from Roman numerals.

Take Ten Fingers

The decimal system uses ten ('deci' is from the Latin word *decimus*, meaning ten) as the base for counting. This makes a lot of sense as people have been counting things on their fingers for thousands of years. It's much more obvious than the Babylonians' base 60 or the Mayans' base 20 systems, for example.

The numbers 1, 2, 3, 4, 5, 6, 7, 8 and 9 are very useful for counting, but the addition of 0 (zero) makes things even simpler. Before zero, if you wanted to keep a record of how many sheep you had, for instance, you might scratch a line on a stick for each one. So if you had three sheep, you'd

scratch three lines: 'III'. However, if you were lucky enough to have 300 sheep, things got tricky, as 300 scratches doesn't look much different to 301 scratches. It also takes a lot of space and a lot of scratching, and what if someone interrupted you after the 288th scratch and you lost count?

The decimal system only takes three symbols to write 300, rather than make 300 scratches. With zero, you can show just how many sheep you have by the position of the numbers – units, tens, hundreds, thousands and so on. Each time you move your number to the left (your three sheep, for instance) and tack a zero on the right, you multiply that number by ten. This way, you can quickly and easily write enormous numbers:

$$3$$
$$30$$
$$300$$
$$3,000$$

Did You Know?

Only in the last few hundred years have people begun to think of zero as a number. It seems odd now, but maths was mainly used for counting *things* for thousands of years. With nothing to count, why would you need a number?

_____A NUMBER OF QUESTIONS_____

You probably already know that a number line is very useful for doing simple calculations. You can easily subtract 3 from 5, just by starting on the 5 and moving 3 numbers to the left, to reach 2:

0 1 2 3 4 5 6 7 8 9 10

A number line also leads to interesting questions, such as, 'What happens to the left of the zero?', 'Where does the line end?' or 'What do the positions between the numbers mean?' All these questions have interesting answers.

To the left of zero are 'negative numbers' (numbers less than zero). If you subtract 5 from 3, you'll get a negative number. Just start at 3 and take 5 steps to the left, to reach −2 (minus 2):

-10 -9 -8 -7 -6 -5 -4 -3 -2 -1 0 1 2 3 4 5 6 7 8 9 10

The number line doesn't come to an end either – it goes on forever. The largest number you could think of can always have a one added to it to make it even bigger. To put it another way, the line goes on to infinity, which is written using the '∞' symbol.

Between the numbers on the number line are fractions, which you'll find out more about on the opposite page.

 COMPARE AND CONTRAST

Ratios, fractions, decimals and percentages are not just useful in maths lessons – you'll also find them very handy when you're out shopping, comparing prices of your favourite toys, for instance.

The Golden Ratio

A ratio compares one thing to another – your eight fingers and two thumbs, for instance, mean that your ratio of fingers to thumbs is 8 to 2, written as 8:2. A ratio that pops up regularly is called the golden ratio. It is roughly 8:13. So if you drew a rectangle measuring 8 cm by 13 cm, it would have the golden ratio and can be called a 'golden rectangle'. It can always be divided into a square and another golden rectangle. If you then draw a curve from one corner to the opposite corner on each square, a spiral will begin to appear (right). It appears in the shapes of many books, buildings, paintings and statues, as people rather like the way that it looks.

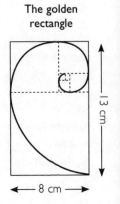

The golden rectangle

13 cm

← 8 cm →

Ratios In Circles

One of the most important ratios you'll come across compares the distance around a circle (the circumference) to the distance across it (the diameter). It is roughly 22:7, or 'pi', written as π – a symbol from the Greek alphabet. You are most likely to use it to find out the area of a circle using the formula $\pi \times r^2$, where 'r' is the radius of the circle.

Fractions And Decimals

Fractions are the things you get if you divide something into smaller parts. Fractions can often be written as ratios, too. For instance, there are seven times as many days in a year as there are weeks. You could say that a day is one seventh of a week, which you can write as the fraction ⅐, or the ratio of weeks to days is 1:7.

Decimals are simply fractions written with numbers after a dot called a decimal point. For example, if you put ⅐ into a calculator (by dividing 1 by 7), it will give you the decimal version of one seventh, which is about 0.142857 going on forever, or 'recurring'. That means you could carry on writing 0.142857142857142857142857 … over and over and over. However, to save space (and paper) you could put dots or lines over the recurring section of numbers, like this: 0.142857 or this: 0.142857.

Some decimals are short and neat, such as a half, which is 0.5 as a decimal. Others are long and neat, like one-third, which is 0.3̇ (recurring). Then there are the long and messy decimals, such as π(3.14159265…), which has no recurring pattern to the numbers after the decimal point, ever.

WEIRD NUMBERS

Although people came up with counting and mathematics, numbers often appear in the natural world, too. Take odd and even numbers for instance. Practically every living thing that has legs has either 2, 4, 6, 8 or some other even number. Flowers, on the other hand, very often have an odd number of petals — five is especially popular (though no-one is sure why). Everything you can see is made up of atoms, which only come in around 100 different types, called elements, each of which has a particular number of particles called protons inside (see page 113).

Triangular Numbers

In ancient Greece, several men with time on their hands seriously enjoyed talking about numbers (oddly, women weren't allowed to do such things then). What they especially liked was to label numbers according to their shapes. Triangular numbers were a particular favourite.

The number ten is a triangular number because it can be arranged into a triangle shape (shown opposite).

So a triangular number is any number you can arrange in a triangle: 1, 3, 6, 10, 15, 21, 28 are all triangular numbers. If you arrange each of the numbers in the sequence into triangle shapes, the bottom row of the next number in the sequence will always have one more dot than on the bottom row of the previous triangle in the sequence.

Square And Cube Numbers

More useful to people today are square numbers, where the number can be arranged in a square shape, like 9:

Each side has 3 dots, so you can say that 9 is 3 'squared' (or $3^2 = 9$), and that 3 is the 'square root' of 9 (or $\sqrt{9} = 3$). It doesn't stop there either. Imagine the dots are sweets (nice sticky ones) and you build a cube out of them. If the cube is 3 sweets high, 3 sweets wide and 3 sweets deep, it contains 27 sweets, so 27 is 3 'cubed' (or $3^3 = 27$). You can check this number by multiplying 3 three times: $3 \times 3 \times 3 = 27$.

Powers

The little number ^{3} in 3^3 is a 'power'. You can have higher powers, too, such as 3^6 or 'three to the power of six'. It's much trickier (impossible, actually) to build from sweets, but easy enough to work out by multiplying six 3s together: $3^6 = 3 \times 3 \times 3 \times 3 \times 3 \times 3 = 729$.

People who are interested in really BIG numbers use a system based on powers of ten. The sun's mass is roughly 2,000,000,000,000,000,000,000,000,000,000 kg, for instance. To save on zeros, this can be written: 2×10^{30} kg, because 10^{30} is the same as 10 multiplied by itself 30 times, which is the same as 1 followed by 30 zeros. This system of writing large numbers is called scientific notation.

MEASURING, TO BE PRECISE

One of the most practical ways to use numbers is for measuring things. Scientists measure most things with what are called SI units (SI stands for *Système International*, which is French for 'International System'). These are a standard set of units that everyone in the world can work from. This means that a kilogram in China, for instance, will be exactly the same as a kilogram in Greenland or Saudi Arabia. There is even a kilogram weight, kept in a vault in Paris, in France, that the weight of all kilograms are based on.

So length is measured in metres (m), area is measured in square metres (m²), volume is measured in cubic metres (m³), mass is measured in kilograms (kg) and time is measured in seconds (s).

One of the best things about SI units is that most of them have smaller and larger versions. The different sizes of unit fit together simply, just by multiplying or dividing by 10, 100 or 1,000. For instance, a kilogram can be divided into grams, or multiplied into metric tonnes. There are 1,000 grams in a kilogram and 1,000 kilograms in a metric tonne.

Taking Measures

By whipping out a tape measure you could, if you wanted, discover how tall your mum is. How easy this is depends on both your mum's patience and how exact you want the measurement to be. Measuring to the nearest decimetre (a decimetre is 10 cm) is very easy – maybe she is 16 decimetres tall. Measuring her height to the nearest centimetre is much more fiddly (162 cm might be the answer). If you tried measuring to the nearest millimetre, things would get very tricky indeed – as often happens when you try to measure things more exactly than anyone needs. You will suddenly find you need to answer a lot of annoying questions such as, 'Should I measure to the top of her hairdo?', 'Should she take her socks off?', 'Does her height change when she breathes in?' and, 'Is this going to take all day?'

The point is, the exactness with which you should make a measurement depends on what you're measuring and why. A flea needs a different unit of measurement to a whale, for instance.

JUMP INTO GEOMETRY

Geometry is the type of maths that looks at shapes, lines and angles. Some shapes, circles for instance, are two dimensional (flat) while others, such as spheres, are three dimensional (solid). Here are a few of the most important two- and three-dimensional shapes and their names:

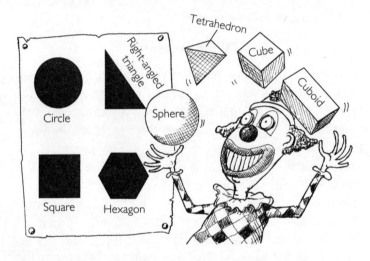

Of course, geometric shapes are not just interesting to mathematicians. Engineers and architects use triangles when they design things because they're rigid and strong. Builders stack cuboids (although they would probably call them bricks) to create walls because they fit together nicely without leaving any gaps. Even bees use geometry, building their hives using hexagons, a shape which uses the smallest possible amount of wax to make a very strong structure.

Geometry is useful to scientists, too. For example, the atoms of different crystals are arranged in different patterns, and this affects the crystals' properties, meaning that they have different characteristics. The atoms in a diamond, for example, are arranged in a pattern of interlocking tetrahedrons and, as a result, it is the world's hardest substance. Graphite is made out of exactly the same stuff as diamonds (carbon). However, the atoms in graphite (the stuff in the middle of your pencil) are arranged in layers of interlocking hexagons, so it is one of the softest substances.

Angles

Angles, measured in degrees (written with the symbol °), are an important part of geometry, too. A full circle has 360° and this is down to the Babylonians, who lived around 4,000 years ago. They loved numbers that 60 could be divided into. (They're the reason we divide hours into 60 minutes, and minutes into 60 seconds).

Right angles are particularly important in geometry. There are four in every rectangle and square, and a right-angled triangle also has one. A right angle is exactly 90°. Angles that are less than 90° are called acute angles. Angles that are more than 90° are obtuse and an angle that is more than 180° is called a reflex angle.

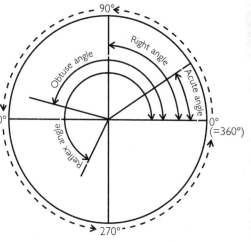

Did You Know?

The angles of the three points of a triangle always add up to 180°, no matter the dimensions of the triangle.

SOME ALGEBRA MAGIC

Algebra is all about using letters (very often x and y) in place of numbers. It's a lot more useful than it sounds. In fact, a lot of scientific discoveries can only be explained with algebra.

For instance, if you fell off a cliff, your speed would gradually increase as the Earth's gravity pulled you towards the ground (or to a nice, safe splashdown in water, hopefully). To while away the journey down, you could work out how fast you are going at any given moment, using a bit of algebra.

You can work out your speed by multiplying the time you have been falling by your acceleration (the rate at which your speed increases). It can be written in an equation like this: $s = t \times a$ (speed equals time multiplied by acceleration).

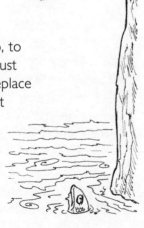

On Earth, things accelerate at about 10 metres per second per second. So, to find out your speed after 2 seconds, just use the numbers that you know to replace letters in the equation. You know that 't' (time) is 2 (the two seconds that you have been falling) and you know that 'a' (acceleration) is 10. So: $s = 2 \times 10 = 20$ metres per second.

Pythagoras' Theorem

Here's a rather nifty equation: $a^2 = b^2 + c^2$. It's called Pythagoras' theorem and it tells you that, in a right-angled triangle, the length of the longest side (the hypotenuse) squared is equal to the lengths of the two shorter sides squared and added together.

For instance, in a right-angled triangle whose shorter sides are 3 cm and 4 cm long, the hypotenuse must be 5 cm long. Here's why:

Imagine 'b' is 3 cm long and 'c' is 4 cm long. If b is squared (b^2), then it will be 3^2. 3×3 equals 9. c must be squared, too (c^2), so it is 4^2. 4×4 equals 16, so, $b^2 + c^2$ is the same as $9 + 16$, which equals 25. Since $a^2 = b^2 + c^2$, that means a^2 must be 25. Now all you need to do is find the square root of 25. 5×5 equals 25, so 5 is the square root of 25 and what's more, it's the length of the hypotenuse, too.

Pythagoras and his followers loved both triangles and numbers. So they were ever so keen on this theorem, until they noticed what happens if the shorter sides of a triangle are, say, both 2 units long. Then the length of the hypotenuse is the square root of $2^2 + 2^2$ – in other words the square root of 8, which is 2.828427. Sadly, the Pythagoreans only liked simple numbers like 1, 2, 3 and so on. They just couldn't cope with messy 'irrational' numbers like 2.828427. They found them so upsetting that they tried to keep them a secret, and even executed one of their friends for talking about them too much.

WHAT ARE THE CHANCES?

Statistics is a very useful kind of maths because it allows you to peer into the future. First you need to collect data (information) about the past and/or the present, after which you have to study it a bit (often by drawing a chart). Then you need to have a bit of a think about what's going on. From this you can make your predictions. Simple.

Say you want to go on holiday to Belgium and avoid the rain. All you need to do is find out how many dry days there were in each of the last 12 months, and draw a chart like the one below, called a histogram or bar chart:

So, the driest month was July.

However, before booking the holiday, you still need to have a little think. You could improve your chances of a good holiday even more by using data from the last 10 years, instead of just the last

12 months, but to do that you need to do some calculations (very easy ones). Here's how:

If, in each January of the last ten years, the numbers of dry days were: 12, 15, 17, 17, 14, 16, 16, 11, 12 and 16, then you can find the average number of dry days per January by adding the days up and dividing by 10. So, 146 ÷ 10 = 14.6. Now, you can round that figure up to 15 days. Do that for each month and you can check whether July is still your best bet for a dry holiday. Even then, July is still only the most promising month – you can't be absolutely certain of staying dry. This is where 'probability' comes in.

Probability

If you know how probable something is, you can give that probability a number. Something certain, such as Monday following Sunday, has a probability of 1. Something impossible, such as living forever, gets a zero, and anything else that *might* happen, has a number in between.

If you toss a coin the probability (or chance) of getting a head is 0.5, which you can call a 1 in 2 probability (because the head is one of only two options). You can also call it a 50:50 probability (if you tossed 100 coins you would get about 50 heads and 50 tails) or a 50% probability.

Unlikely things have small probabilities – the chance of your parents winning the national lottery, for instance, is about 0.00000007, which is about 1 in 14 million.

Did You Know?

How probable is it that two people in the same room have the same birthday? You might expect to need a large group to make it probable, but in fact just 27 people would do.

MATHEMATICAL GREATS

Throughout history, many people have spent a lot of time thinking about maths. Some of them came up with some very useful ideas that we couldn't do without today.

Pythagoras
(Greek, born around 580 BCE, died around 500 BCE)

Not much is known about Pythagoras as he lived such a long time ago. It is not even certain that he came up with the theorem named after him (see page 101), as his followers liked to give him credit for things (plus they were a very secretive bunch). Pythagoras thought that everything, including music, astronomy and nature, could be broken down into numbers.

Archimedes
(Greek, born around 287 BCE, died around 212 BCE)

Archimedes worked out how many grains of sand would fill the universe, a more accurate value for π (see page 93),

and a set of equations that gave the areas and volumes of various shapes. Legend says that he even came up with one theory while he was in the bath, although this is probably not the case. However, he did build war machines to help defend his home city from the Romans, and died during an attack.

Leonardo Fibonacci
(Italian, born around 1170, died around 1250)

Fibonacci described a sequence of numbers in which each number is calculated by adding together the pair of numbers before it (1, 1, 2, 3, 5, 8, 13, 21, 34 and so on). The Fibonacci Sequence, as it's now called, appears naturally in things such as the spiral structures of pineapples, pine cones and sunflower seeds (the seeds grow in spirals, 21 anticlockwise and 34 clockwise).

Fibonacci also promoted the modern decimal system and Hindu-Arabic numerals (see page 89) and proved how much easier it was to do maths with them.

Pierre Fermat
(French, born 1601, died 1665)

Fermat helped to develop theories about probability (see page 103) and made breakthroughs in geometry and the theory of numbers. However, he is probably most famous for jotting down a note in the margin of a book. He wrote that he had solved a particularly tricky problem, but didn't have space to note the answer down just then. This baffled other mathematicians for three centuries, as Fermat never did write down the answer. Finally, with the help of a gigantic computer, an English mathematician and a Canadian physicist were able to work out the solution to the problem Fermat referred to, and published it in 1995.

SCIENCE STUFF

FIRST PHYSICS

Physics is the science that studies the universe and what goes on in it. Physicists are especially interested in matter and energy. Matter is anything that is a solid, a liquid or a gas. Energy is the stuff that allows things to happen: the stuff in a battery that allows a torch to shine, the stuff in nuclear fuel that makes bombs explode, and the stuff in your breakfast that means you can keep going 'til lunch.

Hot On Heat

One especially important type of energy is heat. Heat is actually just molecules (see page 113) wobbling about. The more they wobble, the more heat there is.

Heat moves in three ways, which are demonstrated by this pan of soup:

The soup bubbles, swirls and steams, spreading heat through **convection**.

The pan is hot because heat travels through the metal it is made of by **conduction**.

You can feel the heat from the flames without touching them, because the heat travels to you by **radiation**.

In contrast, cold is just a lack of heat. This means you can't create cold, you can only move heat somewhere else. For instance, the inside of a refrigerator is only cold because the heat is released via the coils of pipe at the back. In fact, refrigerators actually help to warm the rooms they are in.

THE LAWS OF MOTION

Physicists use particular words to describe the way things move. Here's a selection with descriptions of their meanings:

Speed: the distance something moves in a specific amount of time (it is measured in metres per second).
Velocity: speed in a particular direction (metres per second).
Acceleration: the rate of increase in velocity over a specific amount of time (metres per second per second).
Force: the amount of 'push' – the thing which is needed to make an object accelerate or change direction (newtons).
Work: when a force moves an object, 'work' has been done on the object. If you lift a box, the amount of work you do is more the heavier the box is, or the higher you lift it (joules).
Power: the amount of work done in a given time (watts).
Kinetic energy: the energy an object has due to its motion (joules).

Galileo And Newton

An Italian named Galileo sorted out a lot of the physics of motion 400 years ago. He developed scientific theories by doing experiments, rather than just talking about how the world might work, the way the ancient Greeks did.
An Englishman named Isaac Newton then improved on Galileo's theories and came up with these Laws of Motion:

1. Unless forces are applied to them, objects stay in place or keep moving in straight lines without changing velocity.

2. If a force is applied to an object, it will change velocity and direction. The bigger the force, the bigger the change.

3. If you push something, it pushes back just as hard (which is why it hurts your hand if you hit something).

The Ups And Downs Of Waves

Waves are important because they are everywhere, from outer space to the centre of the Earth. There is a special set of words to describe them, too:

Frequency: the number of peaks passing any point (between the two dotted lines, for example) in a second – measured in 'hertz'.
Wavelength: the distance between two identical points.
Peak: the highest point of a wave.
Trough: the lowest point of a wave.

Amplitude: the height of a wave from peak to trough.

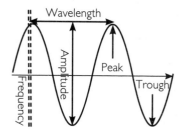

Two of the most well-known waves are light waves and sound waves. They come in handy when you want to see or hear anything, but are very different from each other. The different colours you see are light waves of different frequencies – from low-frequency red through the colours in a rainbow, to high-frequency violet. You hear sound waves of different frequencies as different pitches – the higher the frequency, the higher the note.

A wave of yellow light travels at 299,792,458 metres per second in a vacuum (a completely empty space with no air in it). The length of a wave of light is just 0.00057 mm! Sound waves are very different. For instance, the note middle C on a piano measures 790 mm and travels from the piano to your ear at about 330 metres per second. If you were to place the piano under water, the sound of the notes would actually travel more quickly, at about 1,500 metres per second.

ELECTRICITY AND
 ## MAGNETISM

Electrons (see page 113) are tiny particles which make up the outer layers of atoms, but they can easily be removed. When this happens, these 'free' electrons cause different types of electricity. If they move, along a wire, for instance, they cause an electric current (useful for making lights light up). If they stay in one place, they cause static electricity, which you might hear crackling when you take your pullover off. If you take it off in a dark room, you might even see some flashes and glows, too.

You won't be surprised to hear that magnetism is the property that magnets have. The Earth itself is a huge magnet. Every magnet has two areas called poles – a north pole and a south pole, just like the Earth. Each pole attracts (pulls) poles of the opposite type and repels (pushes away) poles of the same type. This is why the Earth's North Pole attracts the red end of a compass needle, which is the south pole of a little magnet itself.

Electricity and magnetism are closely related – if you send electricity along a wire, the wire becomes slightly magnetic. Likewise, if you wave a magnet about near a wire, a small amount of electricity is created. The area round a magnet where the effects of the magnetism can be detected is called a magnetic field. The area around a charged object is called an electric field. If you put a magnet under a piece of paper and sprinkle iron filings (powdered iron) on it, you can actually see the pattern the magnetic field makes. (You can do without the paper if you don't mind spending the rest of the day picking the iron filings off the magnet.)

SPACE, TIME AND ALL THAT

The fact that planets spin and orbit the sun seems obvious now, but people once believed that the sun was moving around the Earth. Now we know that the reason the sun rises in the east, travels across the sky, and sets in the west is because we are watching it from a spinning planet, but it took absolutely ages for people to work this out (after all, they couldn't just nip up to outer space to have a look).

The Earth rotates, the moon orbits the Earth, and the Earth orbits the sun. These movements give us the lengths of our days, months and years. However, on Neptune, which is much further away from the sun, a year is about 165 times longer than a year on Earth. This is because it takes so much longer for Neptune to orbit the sun. If you lived there, you'd never have a birthday.

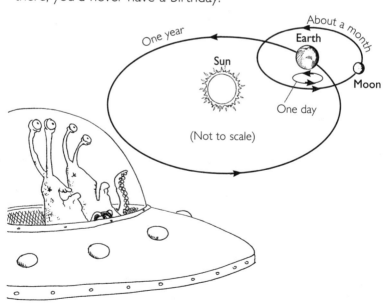

GRAVITY AND BLACK HOLES

Gravity is the force that causes apples to fall to the ground and the moon to move. In fact, every object in the universe pulls on every other object with the force of gravity. The closer objects are together, and the more massive they are, the stronger the pull.

Gravity is usually a weak force – it is only really noticeable when at least one large object, such as the Earth, is involved. The Earth is pretty much spherical in shape – its gravitational pull draws everything towards its centre, making a sphere. However, the spinning of the Earth pushes everything out a little around the equator, so it is a bit like the shape of a slightly squashed ball (called an oblate spheroid, in fact).

Sometimes, however, gravity can be a very strong force indeed. If you had superhuman strength and could crush enough stuff (anything would do) into a tiny volume, you would get so much gravitational force that even light would be sucked in – and create what is called a black hole. If you got too close to a black hole, you would be squeezed by the gravitational force and pulled into a long thin strand – very unpleasant.

Did You Know?

Albert Einstein discovered that strong gravity actually slows the flow of time. This means that if you did lurk about by a black hole for a while, you might find that a century has passed at home, while you had only lived through a year.

QUICK CHEMISTRY

Chemistry is the branch of science that looks at substances called elements and how they react together. Everything in the universe – including the Earth itself and everything on it – is made of 94 different natural elements. (Scientists have learned to make a few more, but most of those go *pffft* and disappear after less than a second.)

Atoms And Molecules

Oxygen, hydrogen, water and your body are all made of tiny particles called atoms. Atoms have a small dense area in the middle – the 'nucleus' – which usually contains a mixture of 'protons' (each with a positive electrical charge) and 'neutrons' (with no electrical charge). Most of an atom is occupied by negatively charged electrons.

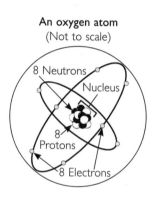

An oxygen atom
(Not to scale)

8 Neutrons
Nucleus
8 Protons
8 Electrons

Often, atoms join together to make 'molecules'. An oxygen molecule is made of two oxygen atoms. A water molecule is made of two hydrogen atoms and one oxygen atom.

In A State

All substances can be divided into solids, liquids or gases (called states or phases). In solids, the atoms or molecules are stuck together, so solids are hard to pull apart. In liquids, they can move past each other, so liquids are runny. In gases, they can get right away from each other, so gases expand to fill whatever container they are in.

Ice, water and water vapour are all the same substance in different phases. To change water from one phase to another, you can change its temperature. For ice (a solid) to turn into water (a liquid), it must be heated until it melts and to turn water into water vapour (a gas), you must heat it until it boils. Usually, ice melts at about 0°C and water boils at about 100°C, however, you could also change the air pressure. For instance, the higher up a mountain you go, the less pressure there is from the Earth's atmosphere (because there is less air pressing down from above), so water will boil at a lower temperature.

Metals Versus Nonmetals

Most of the elements in the universe are metals, and nearly all the rest are nonmetals. Almost all metals and nonmetals can be categorized in the following ways:

Properties	Sample Metals	Sample Nonmetals
	iron, mercury, lead	oxygen, carbon, chlorine
Conducts electricity?	you bet	no chance
Conducts heat?	very well	not very well
Shiny?	usually	usually not
Try twisting a lump of it and…	…it will bend.	…it will snap.

A few elements, such as arsenic and silicon, are neither metal nor nonmetal – these are called metalloids.

Fun Facts

Here are some fascinating facts about elements:

• All living things are based on the element carbon, but the most common element in the universe is hydrogen.

• Planet Earth is made mostly of iron and the air is made mostly of nitrogen (only 21% of the air is oxygen).

• Only mercury and bromine are liquids at room temperature and room pressure.

• It was discovered that helium existed in the sun before it was found on Earth.

• The most expensive element is californium, which costs about a million times as much as gold.

THE PERIODIC TABLE

As there are so many elements and only a few, such as gold, that can be found in a pure form, it took scientists a long time to work out what each one is. A Russian scientist named Dmitri Mendeleyev was a big help with sorting out the elements into the first periodic table, shown below:

1 H																	2 He
3 Li	4 Be											5 B	6 C	7 N	8 O	9 F	10 Ne
11 Na	12 Mg											13 Al	14 Si	15 P	16 S	17 Cl	18 Ar
19 K	20 Ca	21 Sc	22 Ti	23 V	24 Cr	25 Mn	26 Fe	27 Co	28 Ni	29 Cu	30 Zn	31 Ga	32 Ge	33 As	34 Se		
37 Rb	38 Sr	39 Y	40 Zr	41 Nb	42 Mo	43 Tc	44 Ru	45 Rh	46 Pd	47 Cd	48 In	49 Sn	50 Sb	51 Te			
55 Cs	56 Ba	57-70	71 Lu	72 Hf	73 Ta	74 W	75 Re	76 Os	77 Ir			81 Tl	82 Pb	83 Bi	84 Po		
87 Fr	88 Ra	99-102	103 Lr	104 Rf	105 Db	106 Sg	107 Bh	108 Hg	109 Mt	110 Uun		116 Uuq					

57 La	58 Ce	59 Pr	60 Nd	61 Pm	62 Sm	63 Eu	64 Gd	65 Tb
89 Ac	90 Th	91 Pa	92 U	93 Np	94 Pu	95 Am	96 Cm	97 Bk	98 Cf

Mendeleyev noticed that if he arranged the elements he already knew about in order of the weight of their atoms, they formed a pattern. The elements with similar properties were close together. The problem was, the table Dmitri came up with had gaps in it. He decided that there must be elements to fill the gaps, but no one had discovered them yet. Helpfully, he predicted the properties of the missing elements and, sure enough, when new elements were discovered that filled the gaps, these elements had pretty much the properties he had predicted.

An Element's Properties

The periodic table contains all the key facts about each element. Here is a close-up of sodium, one element in the table:

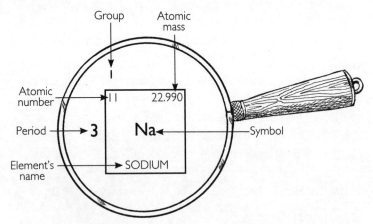

Group. Each column in the table is called a group, numbered from left to right. Elements in the same group all behave in similar ways. Elements in Group 1 are all metals that are very reactive (see opposite). For example, put sodium in water and it rushes about going *fizzzzzzzz*.

Period. Each row on the table is called a period, numbered from top to bottom. The 'reactivity' of elements (see below) changes as you move down the table. For instance, lithium is less reactive than sodium, which is less reactive than potassium, and so on.

Symbol. Each element has a symbol – often the first letter or two of its English name, but this isn't always the case. Sodium's symbol is 'Na' because those are the first two letters of *natrium*, the Latin word for sodium.

Atomic number. This is the number of protons in the element's nucleus (see page 113) and its position in the periodic table.

Atomic mass. This shows the mass of the element's atom, in comparison to the mass of a hydrogen atom (which is 1.0079 atomic mass units).

Elementary Reactions

The electrons that form the outer parts of atoms occupy areas called shells. Each of these shells prefers to have a particular number of electrons in it. For instance, the first shell prefers to contain two electrons. If, as in the case of hydrogen, only one electron is present, the element will be really keen to combine with other elements – in other words, it will be very 'reactive'.

The number of electrons in the outer shells of each element increases from left to right on the table. All the elements in group one have just one electron in their outer shells, so they are all reactive. All the elements in the last group have full shells, so they are very non-reactive.

CHEMICAL COMPOUNDS

Most natural elements are not found in a pure form. They are combined with one or more other elements to make 'compounds'. The type of salt you might sprinkle on your food, for instance, is made from a soft metal called sodium and a poison gas called chlorine – forming what scientists call sodium chloride.

As elements often join up to make compounds, it means that there are many more compounds than elements, and lots of different ways to classify them, including:

Acids, such as citric acid (found in lemon juice) and acetic acid (found in vinegar), like to give away protons and combine with 'bases' (see below) to make salts. Strong acids can even dissolve metal.

Bases, such as ammonia, washing soda and caustic soda like to take up protons (from acids, for example). Bases that dissolve in water are called alkalis.

Organic compounds, such as sugar and vitamins, contain carbon. You are made of organic compounds, too.

Minerals, such as quartz, calcite and diamond, are solids made of particular patterns of chemicals.

Rocks are mixtures of minerals and come in three types: 'igneous' (such as granite), formed from solidified lava; 'sedimentary' (such as limestone), formed when water containing minerals dries; 'metamorphic' (such as marble), formed when one type of rock changes into another.

Chemicals

Chemicals are materials made of one sort of molecule or one pattern of ions (atoms with electrons missing). They have a 'formula', which tells you what their molecules are made of. For instance, sulphuric acid has the formula H_2SO_4 which tells you that its molecules contain two hydrogen atoms (H), one sulphur atom (S) and four oxygen atoms (O). It can also be drawn as a diagram, shown here.

Sulphuric acid

Hydrogen And Oxygen

When you mix two elements together, they usually won't make a compound by themselves. For instance, if you were to open a big bottle of hydrogen, it would just mix with the air around it. However, if you also struck a match, the heat would cause the hydrogen from the bottle to combine with the oxygen in the air to form water.

Water is a compound of hydrogen and oxygen. Its chemical formula is H_2O – two hydrogen atoms and one oxygen atom. However, striking the match would be accompanied by a big explosion, as a result of which you would either be told off or die.

BEGINNERS' BIOLOGY

Biology is the science of living things. But what exactly is a 'living thing'? Fortunately, biologists have sorted out the answer: a living thing must do each of seven specific things.

Seven Signs Of Life

A living thing must **(1) move**, though not necessarily from place to place – if you're a flower, opening your petals will do. It must also **(2) grow** – rather a lot if you're a blue whale, not so much if you're a germ. It must **(3) eat** or get nourishment in some way. A carrot needs sunlight and water, you might eat a carrot, a tiger might eat you – it's all nourishment. This is followed, sooner or later, by going to the toilet (releasing waste gases if you're a carrot) or **(4) 'excreting'** as biologists say. A living thing must also **(5) breathe** – or take in and release gases. For instance, you take some oxygen from the air you breathe in and replace it with carbon dioxide when you breathe out, but plants take in carbon dioxide and release oxygen.

(6) Reproducing (producing offspring) is very useful to avoid dying out. Lastly, a living thing must **(7) react** – if you scream when tickled (or grow more leaves on your sunlit side), it's one more thing that shows you're a living person (or plant).

GETTING UNDER YOUR SKIN

Throughout history, many civilizations have, understandably, been a bit nervous about letting people chop up dead bodies. This meant that it took a long time to work out the basics of human 'anatomy' – that is, what bodies look like inside and how the various bits fit together. Anatomy is only the start of understanding how the human body works though, and even now there is still a lot that is unknown.

Body Systems

As you can see, the body is a complicated living machine. It's made up of various systems, including a digestive system (for eating), a respiratory system (for breathing), a nervous system (for control and communication) and a circulatory system (for moving your blood around).

Each system is made up of organs, which are made of 'tissues'. All tissues are made of tiny building blocks called cells. The largest organ in the circulatory system, for example, is the heart. It's made of a tissue called muscle. It is a blood-pump, which keeps blood flowing around inside you, providing your body with the materials it needs to live and getting rid of wastes, too.

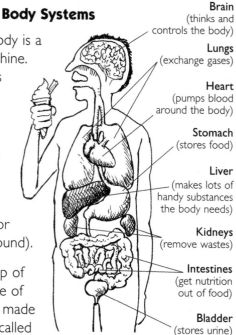

Brain (thinks and controls the body)

Lungs (exchange gases)

Heart (pumps blood around the body)

Stomach (stores food)

Liver (makes lots of handy substances the body needs)

Kidneys (remove wastes)

Intestines (get nutrition out of food)

Bladder (stores urine)

The Human Skeleton

Skull

Clavicle

Scapula

Sternum

Humerus

Vertebrae

Rib

Ulna

Radius

Pelvis

Femur

Patella

Tibia

Fibula

Your skeleton gives you your shape and allows you to move – without one, you'd be a soft, floppy heap. Your bones also help to protect you – for example, your delicate brain and eyeballs are kept safely tucked away inside a strong protective skull. Your muscles pull your bones in various directions, allowing you to walk around and lift things.

Human skeletons are built of over 200 bones, all of which contain a substance called calcium. The points where bones touch are called joints. Many of these joints are flexible – that is, they allow the bones to move. The joints in your elbows and knees are like door hinges, allowing movement in one direction only, but your thigh and shoulder joints allow movement in any direction.

The biggest bone in your body is the 'femur', or thigh bone, and the smallest are the 'ossicles', which are inside your ears. You have three in each ear – each about the size of a rice grain.

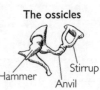

The ossicles

Hammer

Anvil

Stirrup

Did You Know?

Not all living things have skeletons, and many that do wear them on their outsides, like beetles or snails.

MICRO-LIFE

There are millions of trillions of trillions of living things on the Earth. Most of them are too small to see without a microscope – this is why they are called micro-organisms. Most micro-organisms do you no harm at all – which is just as well as they are crawling all over you right now. However, some can make you ill or even kill you. Diseases such as tuberculosis and cholera are caused by micro-organisms called bacteria, which each have only one cell. Colds and flu, however, are caused by 'viruses', which are halfway between living and non-living matter, as they can only reproduce by using the cells of other living things.

The Carbon Cycle

Both you and micro-organisms are involved in what is called the carbon cycle. This system is all about moving carbon around and it keeps us and our world alive. Here's how:

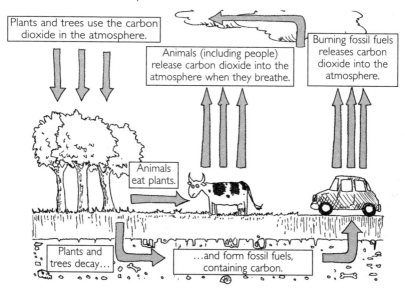

Plants and trees use the carbon dioxide in the atmosphere.

Animals (including people) release carbon dioxide into the atmosphere when they breathe.

Burning fossil fuels releases carbon dioxide into the atmosphere.

Animals eat plants.

Plants and trees decay...

...and form fossil fuels, containing carbon.

WHERE DID YOU COME FROM?

From scorching deserts to freezing mountains, there are many, many different types of habitats on Earth, but the things that live in these places are perfectly suited to their surroundings. How? A process called evolution.

Did You Know?

There's a lot of life running, flapping and crawling about on the planet, and it all started roughly 3.7 billion years ago. Simple chemicals in the seas developed the ability to make copies of themselves. Over millions of years, these chemicals became more complex and joined with others. Eventually, tiny living things formed, each with a single cell. Over time, these creatures developed with different characteristics that helped them fit in with their habitats. So many different living things evolved, that there are now over a million different 'species' (types of living thing) on Earth – and scientists believe that many more are yet to be discovered.

Survival Of The Fittest

Sometimes, living things are born a little different to their parents. If this difference helps them to survive, they will be able to breed and may pass on the difference to their own children. For instance, out of a group of baby lizards born in a sandy area, those that are more sand-coloured are less likely to be seen and eaten by other animals. They will survive and breed, and eventually that type of lizard will be the same colour as the sand.

INDEX